Copyright © 2025 by MJ Woods

All rights reserved.

No portion of this book may be reproduced in any form without written permission from the publisher or author, except as permitted by U.S. copyright law.

Contents

Introduction	1
1. Getting Started with Raised Bed Gardening	3
2. Constructing Your Raised Beds	13
3. Space Optimization Techniques	25
4. Enhancing Garden Aesthetics	35
5. Soil Composition and Health	45
6. Watering Systems and Techniques	55
7. Companion Planting and Crop Rotation	65
8. Natural Pest and Disease Management	75
9. Seasonal Planting and Harvesting	85
10. Building Community and Sharing Knowledge	93
11. Troubleshooting and Problem Solving	103
12. Sustainable Practices for Long-Term Success	111
Conclusion	121
Companion Planting Guide	125

Introduction

Did you know that by growing your own food in a raised bed, you can reduce your carbon footprint and enjoy the freshest, most flavorful produce right from your backyard? It's true! Raised bed gardening is a game-changer for both novice and experienced gardeners alike. It's a fantastic way to maximize your growing space, improve soil quality, and create a thriving, sustainable garden that will keep you harvesting delicious, healthy fruits and veggies all season.

In this book, I'll explain everything you need to know to become a raised bed gardening pro. Whether working with a small balcony or a spacious yard, this all-inclusive guide will provide easy-to-follow techniques and practical advice tailored specifically to raised bed and container gardening.

We'll dive into the nitty-gritty of building your raised beds using various materials catering to different skill levels and budgets. You'll learn how to create the perfect soil composition to give your plants the best possible start and keep them thriving throughout the growing season. I'll also share secrets to companion planting that will help you maximize your garden's health and productivity.

But that's not all! We'll explore efficient watering systems and techniques to help ensure your plants get the hydration they need without wasting a drop. You'll discover natural pest and disease management strategies that keep your garden looking its best without harmful chemicals. And because every region has its own unique gardening challenges, I'll provide climate-specific guidance to help you succeed no matter where you live.

One of the best things about raised bed gardening is that it allows you to grow more food in less space. Even if you only have a few square feet to work with, you can enjoy abundant fresh produce by utilizing vertical growing techniques and smart plant spacing. The improved soil drainage and aeration in raised beds mean healthier plants and bigger harvests.

Throughout this book, I'll share tips and tricks to save you time, money, and effort as you create your dream garden. From cost-effective solutions for building your raised beds to crop rotation strategies that keep your soil nutrient-rich, you'll find everything you need to succeed as a raised bed gardener.

So, whether you're a seasoned green thumb looking to take your gardening to the next level or a complete beginner who's always wanted to grow your own food but didn't know where to start, "The Raised Bed Gardening Handbook" is here to help. Get ready to roll up your sleeves, dig in, and discover the joys of creating a beautiful, bountiful, raised bed garden that nourishes your body and soul. Let's get growing!

Chapter One

Getting Started with Raised Bed Gardening

Have you ever walked past a neighbor's garden and thought, "Wow, how do they manage to grow so much in such a small space?" Raised bed gardening is often the secret behind those lush, overflowing plots. It's not just about aesthetics; it's a smart gardening strategy that offers numerous benefits. Whether you're trying to squeeze a garden into a tiny urban yard or looking to make your gardening efforts more efficient, raised beds are your ticket to success. As we dig into this chapter, you'll see why raised beds are a top choice for gardeners everywhere and how they can transform your gardening experience.

Understanding the Benefits of Raised Bed Gardening

Raised bed gardening isn't just a trend—it's a revolutionary approach that enhances your gardening efforts in many ways. One of the standout advantages is improved soil drainage and aeration. By elevating the soil, raised beds prevent water logging, which is a common issue in traditional gardens, especially during heavy rains. This elevation also allows for better airflow around the plant roots, promoting healthier plant growth. With the ability to control the soil quality, you can easily amend and enrich the soil, ensuring your plants have the nutrients they need to thrive. Moreover, the soil in raised beds warms up quicker in the spring, allowing you to extend your growing season and get a jump start on planting.

Another fantastic perk of raised beds is the ease of pest control and management. The defined structure of these beds makes it simple to implement natural pest control measures, such as using row covers or diatomaceous earth. Raised beds create a physical barrier that deters certain pests, reducing the need for harmful pesticides and promoting a balanced ecosystem. This aligns perfectly with sustainable gardening practices, helping you grow healthier and more resilient plants.

Raised beds also make gardening more accessible for everyone. The elevated design reduces the need to bend or kneel, which is a massive benefit if you have back or mobility issues. You can customize the height of your beds to suit your needs, making gardening a more comfortable and enjoyable activity. This accessibility opens up the gardening world to more people, encouraging those who might have thought it was out of reach to get their hands dirty and nurture their plants.

In terms of productivity, raised beds are incredibly efficient. The ability to plant intensively means growing more in less space, which is ideal for urban and suburban gardeners with limited room. By carefully planning your planting layout, you can maximize yield while minimizing maintenance. Raised beds allow you to implement companion planting strategies that enhance plant health and productivity, effectively using every inch of available space.

Beyond the practical advantages, raised beds offer aesthetic and community benefits. They're customizable to fit any landscape, allowing you to design a garden that reflects your personal style. Whether you prefer a rustic look with wood frames or a sleek modern design with metal, raised beds can adapt to your vision. They also provide opportunities for community gardening projects, fostering collaboration and sharing among local gardeners. Raised beds can become a focal point in your neighborhood, bringing people together and creating a shared space for learning and growth.

When deciding if raised bed gardening is right for you, consider your goals, resources, and constraints. Think about the space you have available, your physical abilities, and your gardening aspirations. Raised beds offer flexibility, allowing you to tailor your garden to meet your specific needs. Whether you want to grow a few herbs on a balcony or cultivate a full vegetable garden, raised beds can accommodate your plans and help you achieve the garden of your dreams.

Choosing the Perfect Location for Your Raised Beds

Picture this: a thriving garden brimming with vibrant vegetables and colorful blooms. It all starts with choosing the right spot. Location is everything when it comes to raised bed gardening, and several factors must be considered to ensure success. First and foremost, sunlight is key. To flourish, most vegetables and flowers require a good six to eight hours of direct sunlight each day. Before settling on a location, observe your outdoor space at different times of the day to track the sun's path. This will help you identify the sunniest spots, ensuring your plants get the light they need to grow strong and healthy. Suppose your garden is shaded by large trees or buildings. In that case, you might need to reposition your beds to take advantage of the available sunlight or consider growing shade-tolerant plants.

Proximity to a water source is another critical factor. Dragging a heavy hose across your yard can quickly become a chore, so placing your raised beds within easy reach of a faucet is wise. This convenience makes watering your garden a breeze. Pay attention to existing trees and shrubs as well. Their extensive root systems can compete with your garden plants for nutrients and water, so it's best to avoid placing your beds too close to them.

Environmental elements also play a significant role in site selection. Strong winds can damage delicate plants, so consider using natural windbreaks like fences or hedges to shield your garden. Understanding your yard's natural slope and drainage patterns is also essential. Raised beds should be placed on level ground to prevent water from pooling and causing root rot. If your garden has a slight slope, orient the beds perpendicular to the hill to facilitate even water distribution. Additionally, be mindful of temperature variations. Gardens in valleys or low-lying areas might experience frost pockets, while those on slopes may warm up faster in spring.

Now, let's talk aesthetics. Your raised beds should be functional but can also be a beautiful addition to your landscape. Think of them as blank canvases where you can express your creativity. Consider the overall design and flow of your garden. Raised beds can be used to create symmetry or add structure to a more naturalistic setting. Choose materials and colors that complement your existing outdoor decor. The possibilities are endless, whether you prefer rustic wood, sleek metal, or colorful stone. Integrating your raised beds with the surrounding environment will create a harmonious garden that pleases the eye and the palate.

Of course, every garden comes with its fair share of challenges. Shading from nearby structures is a common obstacle. If you encounter this, try positioning your beds to capture morning light, which is often less obstructed. Uneven ground can also pose a problem, but it's nothing a little creativity can't fix. Consider building tiered beds or using leveling techniques to establish stability. And if space is tight, container gardening is a fantastic alternative. A sunny patio or balcony can be transformed into a productive garden with a few well-placed pots and planters. Container gardening offers similar benefits to raised beds. It can be tailored to fit any space, making it an excellent option for urban dwellers.

Quick Exercise: Map Your Garden:

Grab a notebook and sketch out your garden space. Mark areas that receive the most sunlight and note any shady spots. Consider water access and potential obstacles like trees and buildings. Use this map to visualize where your raised beds or containers will thrive best. This exercise will help you make informed decisions about your garden layout and help you choose the optimal location for your raised beds.

Essential Tools and Materials for Beginners

Embarking on your raised bed gardening adventure requires the right tools. Think of them as your trusty companions, ready to help you transform that patch of soil into a thriving oasis. Let's begin with the basics: hand tools. A sturdy trowel is indispensable for digging, planting, and transferring soil. It fits comfortably in your hand and is perfect for those intricate tasks around your plants. Pair this with a hand fork, which is excellent for loosening soil and removing pesky weeds. And don't forget a pair of sharp pruners. They allow you to prune plants with precision, keeping them healthy and encouraging growth. Whether snipping off dead leaves or harvesting herbs, pruners are a must-have.

Next up are shovels and hoes, the workhorses of any garden. A good shovel is essential for moving soil, compost, and other materials. It helps you shape and fill your raised beds with ease. Meanwhile, a hoe is perfect for breaking up clumps of soil and creating furrows for planting seeds. These tools might seem straightforward, but their utility in preparing and maintaining your garden can't be overstated. They make the heavy lifting of gardening more manageable, ensuring you're ready to tackle any task that comes your way.

Watering is another critical part of the gardening process, and having the right equipment makes all the difference. A watering can with a rose attachment or a hose with an adjustable nozzle gives you control over water flow, allowing you to gently water delicate seedlings or drench thirsty plants on hot days. These tools are essential for your garden to receive the right amount of hydration without disturbing the soil or splashing leaves— the key to preventing disease. By carefully managing your watering, you set the stage for robust plant growth.

For those looking to elevate their gardening game, consider adding optional tools to your arsenal. Drip irrigation kits, for instance, can save you time and water. These systems deliver water directly to the plant roots, reducing waste and ensuring consistent moisture levels. They're particularly beneficial if you travel often or have a busy schedule, as they can be set on timers to water your garden automatically. This precision watering helps keep your plants healthy and frees you up to focus on other gardening tasks.

Another valuable tool is a soil tester. Understanding your soil's pH and nutrient levels is critical for optimal plant health. A simple soil test can tell you what your soil might lack, guiding you on what amendments to add. Whether your soil needs more lime to raise the pH or some extra compost to boost nutrients, a soil tester provides the information you need to make informed decisions. This knowledge guarantees your plants have the best possible environment to thrive.

As you gather your tools, remember that quality matters. Investing in durable, reliable equipment can save you time and frustration in the long run. While going for the cheapest option can be tempting, a well-made tool will last longer and perform better. Consider it an investment in your garden's future. With the right tools at your side, you're well-equipped to tackle any gardening challenge, from planting the first seed to harvesting the fruits of your labor.

Planning Your Garden Layout for Maximum Efficiency

Pathways wide enough to maneuver a wheelbarrow.

Strategic planning of your raised bed garden layout is like crafting a masterpiece. Every plant has its place, and every path has its purpose. Thoughtful layout design isn't merely about aesthetics; it influences productivity and ease of access, making gardening a more enjoyable and fruitful endeavor. Imagine a garden where every plant is within reach, and each path invites you to explore further. Pathways are essential in this setup. They provide easy access to your plants and help prevent soil compaction by directing foot traffic away from your growing areas. Whether you opt for gravel, mulch, or stepping stones, pathways should be wide enough for comfortable navigation, allowing you to tend to your plants without disturbing the soil or causing damage.

Now, let's talk about maximizing space. It's all about making the most of what you have. Picture a jigsaw puzzle where each piece fits perfectly. In your garden, this means arranging plants to complement their growth habits and requirements. Companion planting is an excellent strategy for optimizing space and enhancing plant health. You can create a harmonious environment that boost productivity by pairing plants that benefit each other, like tomatoes with basil or carrots with onions. Consider plant height and spread when planning your layout. Taller plants can provide shade for sun-sensitive companions.

At the same time, those with sprawling habits can fill in gaps, making efficient use of every inch.

To further enhance your garden's output, incorporate succession and rotation planning. These techniques keep your soil healthy and your harvests continuous. Planning for crop rotation involves changing the types of plants grown in a particular area each season, which prevents nutrient depletion and reduces pest and disease buildup. Succession planting, on the other hand, involves staggering plantings of the same crop to provide a constant supply. Imagine enjoying fresh lettuce from spring through fall by sowing new seeds every few weeks. These methods maintain soil fertility and maximize your garden's productivity throughout the year.

Succession Planting - Crops planted several weeks apart to provide a continuous supply.

While functionality is key, don't overlook the aesthetic aspect of your garden layout. A well-designed garden is a feast for the eyes as well as the stomach. Consider whether you prefer symmetrical designs, which offer a sense of order and balance, or asymmetrical layouts that provide a more natural, dynamic look. Play with color and texture to create visual interest. You might plant vibrant flowers alongside leafy greens or use different leaf shapes and sizes to add depth. By thoughtfully arranging plants, you can create a garden that delights the senses and enhances your outdoor space.

As you plan your garden, remember that it reflects your personality and creativity. Your layout should not only be efficient but also bring you joy and satisfaction. Take the time to sketch out your ideas, experiment with different arrangements, and adjust as needed. The beauty of gardening lies in its flexibility and endless opportunities for learning and growth. Whether working with a small urban plot or a sprawling backyard, a well-planned layout can transform any space into a productive, beautiful haven.

In conclusion, planning your raised bed garden layout is an art that balances practicality with creativity. By considering access, space efficiency, and visual appeal, you can create a garden that is both functional and beautiful. Embrace the process, and enjoy the satisfaction of watching your carefully planned garden flourish season after season.

Chapter Two

Constructing Your Raised Beds

I magine your garden as a blank canvas, and you hold the brush. The materials you choose for your raised beds will define the look, longevity, and environmental impact of your garden. Selecting the right material is a foundational step in creating a beautiful and enduring garden. Let's explore the options, weighing the benefits and drawbacks of each, so you can make an informed decision that suits your style and needs.

Wood remains a favorite for many gardeners due to its natural appearance and versatility. If you're seeking durability, cedar and redwood stand out for their natural rot resistance. These woods have oils that deter decay, making them ideal for long-term use. However, they can be pricier than other options. Pine, on the other hand, is more budget-friendly but lacks inherent protection against the elements. If you choose pine, consider applying a non-toxic wood treatment to extend its lifespan.

Metal, mainly galvanized steel, offers a modern aesthetic and robust durability. This material resists rust and can withstand harsh weather, giving you peace of mind that your raised beds will last. Metal beds warm up quickly in the sun, extending your growing season by allowing earlier planting. Metal could be your perfect match if you want something that combines strength with style. Remember that the initial investment might be higher, but the longevity of metal can outweigh the upfront costs.

Stone brings a timeless, classic feel to your garden. Imagine beds crafted from natural stone, offering not just a planting area but a statement piece in your landscape. Stone is unmatched in durability and can last for decades without much maintenance. However, it can be heavy and more challenging to work with, requiring a significant initial investment and effort. If you're drawn to the charm and permanence of stone and don't mind the labor, it can be a rewarding choice.

When considering materials, it's essential to think about environmental impact. Recycled timber is a sustainable option that reduces waste and repurposes existing resources. This choice supports the environment while offering rustic beauty. Additionally, sourcing materials locally minimizes transportation emissions and supports the local economy. These considerations benefit the planet and enhance the story and connection you have with your garden.

Budget is another important factor. Compare the costs of materials based on their purchase price, longevity, and maintenance requirements. While cedar and stone might have higher initial costs, their durability can make them cost-effective in the long run. Pine or recycled timber might be more affordable upfront but require frequent replacement or treatment. Understanding these trade-offs will help you choose a material that aligns with your financial constraints without compromising on quality.

Maintenance and longevity are closely tied to the material you select. While more affordable, Untreated woods may not stand up to the elements over time. They require regular maintenance, such as sealing or staining, to prolong their life. On the other hand, Treated options offer greater resilience with less ongoing care. However, always make sure that any treatments used are safe for growing food to avoid chemical leaching into your soil.

Exercise: Material Selection Checklist

Create a checklist to help you decide which material best suits your needs. Consider factors such as budget, aesthetics, environmental impact, and maintenance. Rank these criteria in order of importance to you, and use this list as a guide to evaluate each material option.

As you navigate these decisions, remember that your choice of material will shape your garden's character and functionality. By thoughtfully considering each option's benefits and challenges, you can construct raised beds that not only serve as a practical solution for growing plants but also enhance the beauty and sustainability of your outdoor space.

Step-by-Step Guide to Building Wooden Raised Beds

Starting from scratch might seem daunting, but building your own wooden raised beds can be a rewarding project. Imagine the satisfaction of crafting a sturdy, beautiful bed ready to host your garden dreams. Follow these step-by-step instructions to ensure your project is a success:

Step 1: Choose Your Lumber

Begin by selecting your wood. Avoid treated wood, as it may contain chemicals that can leach into the soil. Visit your local hardware store and pick planks that are straight, free of cracks, and appropriate for the dimensions of your raised bed.

Step 2: Plan and Measure

Decide on the size and shape of your raised bed. A typical size is 4 feet wide by 8 feet long, as this allows you to reach the center from either side without stepping into the bed. Aim for a height of 12 to 18 inches, which provides ample depth for root growth while keeping maintenance manageable.

Use a measuring tape and pencil to mark your lumber. Measure twice to ensure precision and minimize waste. For a 4'x8' bed that is 12 inches tall, you'll need two planks (6 inches wide) cut to 8 feet for the long sides and two planks (6 inches wide) cut to 4 feet for the shorter ends.

Step 3: Cut the Boards

Using a circular saw, hand saw, or miter saw, carefully cut the boards to the marked dimensions. If you're unfamiliar with power tools, prioritize safety:

- Wear safety goggles and gloves.
- Use clamps to secure the lumber while cutting.
- Work on a stable surface and "measure twice, cut once".

Step 4: Drill Pilot Holes

To prevent the wood from splitting, drill pilot holes where you'll insert screws or bolts. Place holes about 1 inch from the edge of the boards and evenly spaced along the length. For each corner, plan for at least two screws or bolts to provide sufficient stability.

Step 5: Assemble the Frame

Lay out the boards in the shape of your desired bed—a rectangle or square. Start assembling one corner at a time:

1. Position the boards at a 90-degree angle.

2. Use a drill to attach the boards with screws, ensuring they're tight and secure.

3. For added strength, use metal corner braces. Align each brace inside the corner, and fasten it with screws. This will reinforce the joints and help your bed withstand the pressure of soil and water.

Repeat the process for all four corners, constantly checking that the corners are square using a carpenter's square or measuring diagonals for equal lengths.

Step 6: Check for Level and Stability

Once the frame is assembled, place it in its intended location. Use a spirit level to ensure the bed sits evenly on the ground. If the ground is uneven, remove a small amount of soil to create a flat surface. A level bed ensures water distributes evenly and prevents soil from washing out over time. An uneven foundation can lead to water pooling in certain areas, potentially damaging plants. Proper drainage is equally important; without it, water can accumulate, leading to root rot and plant failure. Consider adding a layer of gravel or sand at the base of your bed to improve drainage, allowing excess water to escape and keeping your plants healthy.

Step 7: Prepare the Base

If you're placing the bed on bare ground, consider lining the base with hardware cloth or chicken wire to deter burrowing pests. Secure the wire to the bottom of the frame using a staple gun. For added weed prevention, lay down a layer of landscape fabric over the wire before adding soil.

Step 8: Fill the Bed

Fill your raised bed with a nutrient-rich mix of soil. Use the information in chapter five to create the ideal mix.

Customization allows you to tailor your raised beds to your specific needs. Consider adding height to your beds if you prefer gardening without bending or kneeling. This is particularly beneficial for those with mobility challenges, transforming gardening into an accessible and comfortable activity. Incorporating trellises offers a vertical growing option for those looking to maximize space. Climbing plants like beans or cucumbers can thrive, using the trellis for support and freeing up ground space for other crops. Customization not only enhances functionality but also adds a personal touch, reflecting your unique gardening style.

As you immerse yourself in the construction process, remember that each step brings you closer to a thriving garden. Building your own raised bed is more than just assembling wood; it's about creating a nurturing environment for your plants. With careful planning and attention to detail, your raised bed will become a welcoming home for your garden's bounty.

DIY Alternatives: Using Recycled and Upcycled Materials

Have you ever looked at old pallets and thought they could be more than just discarded wood? With a bit of creativity and elbow grease, these humble materials can transform into charming and functional raised beds. Pallets offer a rustic, cost-effective solution for those who want to give gardening a try without breaking the bank. They are often readily available, sometimes even for free, from local businesses. When using pallets, it's essential to make sure they're safe for gardening by checking for any harmful chemical treatments. Look for the "HT" stamp, indicating they were heat-treated rather than chemically treated. This simple precaution protects your soil and plants from potential contamination.

Concrete blocks present another intriguing option. With their modern, industrial look, they can bring a contemporary edge to your garden. These blocks are not only durable but also easy to stack and configure into various shapes and sizes. They provide excellent insulation for your beds, helping to maintain stable soil temperatures. Plus, they allow for flexibility; you can move and rearrange them to suit your garden's evolving needs. Consider planting smaller herbs and flowers in the hollow spaces of the blocks to add visual interest and maximize your growing area. This approach combines form and function, creating a unique garden space that reflects your style.

Using recycled materials for your raised beds offers significant environmental benefits. By repurposing items that might otherwise end up in a landfill, you reduce waste and contribute to a more sustainable world. This practice not only lowers your carbon footprint but also encourages a mindset of resourcefulness and creativity. It's satisfying to know you're giving new life to old materials while creating a productive garden. This sustainable approach aligns with the broader goal of eco-conscious living, showing that small changes can have a big impact.

THE RAISED BED GARDENING HANDBOOK 21

When constructing a raised bed with concrete blocks, start by planning your layout. Arrange the blocks on a level surface, stacking them securely. The weight of the blocks will naturally hold them in place, but for added stability, you can use construction adhesive between layers. Assure the bed is square or rectangular to provide a stable foundation for your plants. Once the structure is complete, fill it with your chosen soil mix and start planting. The solid nature of concrete blocks makes them resistant to weathering, providing a long-lasting solution for your garden needs.

Working with pallets requires a bit more preparation. Begin by disassembling the pallet boards using a pry bar or saw. This process may take some time, but it's important to work carefully to avoid splitting the wood. Once you have separated the boards, sand down any rough edges to prevent splinters. Assemble the boards into a rectangular or square frame, securing them with nails or screws. For added strength, use corner braces to reinforce the joints. Before filling your bed with soil, line the inside with landscape fabric to prevent soil from escaping and add a barrier against weeds.

While the use of non-traditional materials is innovative, it comes with its own set of challenges. Ensuring the structural integrity of your raised beds is critical, especially when using recycled materials. Check that all components are securely fastened and stable before adding soil and plants. As previously mentioned, it's important to address possible chemical contamination. Avoid pallets exposed to toxic substances or show signs of significant wear. By taking these precautions, you can enjoy the benefits of recycled materials in your garden safely and responsibly.

Designing Aesthetic Raised Beds for Your Garden

Designing your raised beds is a unique opportunity to bring a touch of artistry to your garden. Imagine selecting plants not just for their taste or yield but for their colors and textures, creating a living tapestry that changes with the seasons. Start by considering how different plants can complement each other visually. For instance, pairing deep green kale with the silver leaves of sage can create a striking contrast, while bright marigolds can add a pop of color against a backdrop of leafy greens. Balance is key; think about how plants will look together, whether you're aiming for a harmonious blend of colors or a bold, contrasting palette.

The structure of your raised beds can also significantly influence the overall design. Symmetry can evoke a sense of order and calm, ideal for a formal garden setting. On the other hand, asymmetrical designs might offer a more dynamic and natural feel, perfect for a whimsical, cottage-style garden. When planning these arrangements, consider the height and spread of your plants. Tall plants like sunflowers can serve as focal points, while ground-hugging herbs can cascade over the edges, softening the lines of your beds.

Decorative elements like edging materials and finishes can further enhance the visual appeal of your raised beds. Stones or tiles can add a classic touch, providing a neat border that defines the space. If you prefer a splash of color, consider painting or staining the wood of your beds. A rich, earthy stain can enhance the natural beauty of the wood, while a bold color can make your garden stand out. These finishing touches are the jewelry of your garden, adding detail and interest that draw the eye and create coherence across your space.

Integration with existing landscapes is another layer to consider. Your raised beds should complement the existing features of your garden, such as pathways, fences, or patios. By matching materials and colors with these features, you create a cohesive look that ties the whole garden together. Position your beds to accentuate existing lines and structures, perhaps using them to frame a view or create a welcoming entrance. This thoughtful placement enhances both the beauty and functionality of your outdoor space.

Personal expression is where your raised bed garden truly becomes your own. Think of your garden as a canvas where you can reflect your style and creativity. Maybe you want to add personal art or sculptures to your garden, incorporating elements that resonate with your tastes and experiences. Seasonal plant arrangements can also keep your garden dynamic and fresh throughout the year. Imagine a bed that bursts with tulips in the spring, transitions to lush vegetables in the summer, and concludes with vibrant asters in the fall. This approach showcases your personality and encourages continual engagement with your garden.

As you design your raised beds, remember that they are more than just functional. They are an extension of your home and a reflection of your personality. By balancing color and texture, using decorative finishes, integrating with existing landscapes, and adding personal touches, you create a garden that is uniquely yours. Each choice you make contributes to a space that is as inviting as it is productive, a place where you can relax, experiment, and grow.

Chapter Three

Space Optimization Techniques

Have you ever wished you could grow more plants in less space? It's a common dilemma for many gardeners, especially when working with limited square footage. That's where vertical gardening comes in—a creative solution that allows you to grow upward instead of outward, effectively multiplying your planting area. Think of it as taking your garden to the next level, literally. By embracing vertical gardening, you can transform even the smallest patch of land into a lush, productive oasis. It's like building a skyscraper for your plants, where every inch counts and the sky's the limit.

Vertical gardening in raised beds is an ingenious way to maximize your growing potential. Imagine using trellises and cages to train climbing plants like cucumbers and pole beans to reach the sky. These structures provide support as the plants ascend, freeing up horizontal space for other crops. Trellises can be made from simple materials like bamboo or metal stakes, offering both functionality and aesthetics. As your climbing plants flourish, they create a living wall of greenery, adding depth and dimension to your garden. But the benefits don't stop there. Vertical gardening also opens up opportunities for wall-mounted planters, perfect for herbs and flowers. These planters can be attached to fences or garden walls, bringing color and fragrance to eye level where they're easily accessible.

Choosing the right plants is essential for a successful vertical garden. Climbing plants like cucumbers and pole beans are natural choices, as they thrive when given the opportunity to grow upwards. Their long vines eagerly wrap-around supports, producing abundant yields in a compact space. Strawberries, when grown in hanging baskets, provide another excellent option. These baskets can be suspended from hooks or placed on tiered shelves, making harvesting as easy as picking ripe berries at arm's length. The beauty of vertical gardening lies in its versatility, allowing you to experiment with different plant combinations and arrangements to suit your space and taste.

Constructing vertical supports doesn't have to be a daunting task. Start with a simple trellis made from bamboo, a sustainable and affordable material. Bamboo stakes can be arranged in a teepee or fan shape, providing a sturdy framework for your plants. Alternatively, metal stakes offer a sleek, modern look and can be arranged to create intricate designs. Those interested in a DIY project should consider designing tiered shelves for small pots. These shelves can be constructed from wood or repurposed materials, creating a multi-level platform for your plants. This approach maximizes space and adds visual interest to your garden.

The benefits of vertical gardening extend beyond mere space-saving. Elevating plants improves air circulation, which helps reduce the risk of diseases by keeping foliage dry and healthy. This elevation also makes maintenance and harvesting more manageable, as you can access your plants without bending or stretching. Imagine walking through your garden, plucking ripe tomatoes or fragrant herbs without straining your back. It's a gardener's dream come true, offering both convenience and efficiency. Vertical gardening invites you to think outside the box and explore new dimensions in your gardening practice.

Exercise: Vertical Garden Sketch

Grab a sketchpad and pencil. Draw your garden space and envision where vertical elements could fit. Note potential spots for trellises, cages, and wall-mounted planters. Consider the sunlight each area receives and how this might affect plant growth. This exercise will help you visualize your vertical garden and guide your planning process, ensuring you make the most of every square inch.

Square Foot Gardening for Maximized Space

Imagine transforming your garden into a neatly organized grid, where every plant has its own designated space, and every inch of soil is put to good use. That's the beauty of square-foot gardening. This method maximizes your raised bed area by dividing it into one-foot sections, creating a checkerboard of possibilities. Picture a garden where each square foot is like a mini garden bed, carefully planned and planted with precision. This approach makes your garden look tidy and ensures that each plant gets exactly what it needs to thrive.

Planning a grid layout is the first step to embracing square-foot gardening. Using string or wood dividers, you mark each square foot within your raised bed. This grid acts as your guide, helping you plan which plants to grow and where to place them. For high-yield crops like lettuce and radishes, you can plant them densely within a single square, reaping the benefits of multiple harvests from a small space. Given their sprawling nature, larger plants like tomatoes might require an entire square or even multiple squares. The grid helps you visualize your planting strategy, ensuring that every plant has adequate room to grow while maximizing your garden's productivity.

Choosing the right plants and spacing them correctly is essential to the success of this method. High-yield, fast-growing crops such as lettuce, radishes, and spinach can be planted closely together, taking advantage of their compact growing habits to fill each square with lush greenery. This dense planting increases your yield and reduces weed growth by shading the soil, making maintenance easier. For larger plants, like tomatoes or peppers, you allocate more space. These plants need room to spread out and absorb sunlight, so giving them their own square or even multiple squares guarantees they have the space to flourish.

The benefits of square-foot gardening are numerous, making it a favorite among gardeners looking to increase their garden's efficiency and productivity. The dense planting pattern naturally suppresses weeds, saving you time and effort in maintenance. This method also simplifies planting and harvesting schedules. By organizing your garden into a grid, you can easily see which squares need attention, whether planting, watering, or harvesting. This clarity makes it easier to manage your garden, even if you're juggling a busy schedule. Additionally, square-foot gardening promotes healthy soil by encouraging crop rotation within the grid. By moving plants to different squares each season, you prevent soil depletion and break pest and disease cycles. This practice keeps your soil healthy and your garden productive year after year. With square-foot gardening, you have a method that maximizes space and streamlines your gardening efforts, allowing you to enjoy a bountiful harvest with minimal fuss.

Implementing square-foot gardening in your raised beds is straightforward and rewarding. Start by using string or wood slats to create a visible grid on your bed. This grid will serve as your blueprint, guiding your planting decisions.

Intercropping Strategies for Small Gardens

In the dance of nature, intercropping is a technique where harmony and efficiency reign supreme. Imagine your garden as a vibrant tapestry, with each plant playing its part in a larger symphony. Intercropping involves growing multiple crops in the same space, allowing them to interact and support one another. This method optimizes the use of resources, like sunlight and water, by pairing fast-growing crops with those that take their time. Integrating tall plants with shorter ones creates a layered effect—like a forest within your garden—where each plant thrives in its niche. This approach isn't just about cramming more plants into a small space; it's about creating a living ecosystem that works in balance.

When it comes to selecting the perfect plant combinations for intercropping, think of it as matchmaking for your plants. Some pairings are like classic duos that just work well together. Take, for instance, the "Three Sisters" method, which Indigenous peoples have used for centuries. In this trio, corn, beans, and squash are planted together. The corn provides a natural trellis for the beans to climb; the beans fix nitrogen in the soil, enriching it for all three, and the squash sprawls along the ground, shading out weeds and keeping the soil moist. Another effective pairing is lettuce and radishes. Lettuce grows relatively slowly but spreads out, while radishes are quick to mature. By the time your radishes are ready to harvest, the lettuce is just hitting its stride, allowing for a seamless transition and continuous use of the space.

The benefits of intercropping extend beyond efficient space utilization. This approach enhances soil nutrient use, as different plants often have varying nutrient needs and root depths. Growing them together reduces competition and better utilizes the available resources. Intercropping can also help reduce soil erosion, as the dense plant cover protects the soil from heavy rain and wind. Another significant advantage is natural pest deterrence. A diverse planting scheme can confuse pests, making finding and attacking their target plants harder. Additionally, certain plant combinations can attract beneficial insects that prey on common garden pests, creating a natural defense system.

For those of you working with limited space, making intercropping work requires a bit of planning and creativity. Start by considering the growth habits and needs of each plant. Planning crop succession is key to maintaining continuous growth. As one crop matures and is harvested, another can be sown in its place, ensuring your garden is always productive. Companion planting charts can be invaluable, providing guidance on which plants work well together and which should be kept apart. These charts take the guesswork out of plant selection, allowing you to focus on cultivating a thriving, balanced garden.

Intercropping isn't just a practical technique; it's an invitation to experiment and learn from nature. By observing how plants interact and support each other, you better understand the ecosystem you're nurturing. This approach turns your garden into a dynamic and interconnected space where every plant has a role to play. As you explore intercropping, you'll discover the joy of seeing different crops flourish side by side, each contributing to the health and vitality of your garden. Embrace the challenge of intercropping, and watch as your small garden transforms into a bustling hub of biodiversity and productivity.

Designing Multi-Level Raised Bed Systems

Have you ever considered transforming your garden into a dynamic and visually stunning space that maximizes planting area and adds an artistic flair? Multi-level raised bed systems might just be the answer. By staggering raised beds in tiers or incorporating steps and terraces on sloped terrain, you can create a garden that flows naturally with the landscape while offering a variety of planting zones. This approach is particularly useful in hilly areas with limited flat gardening surfaces.

By embracing the natural contours of your garden, you create a tiered effect that not only maximizes space but also makes access easier, as each level can be reached without excessive bending or stretching.

Plant selection is crucial in ensuring that each layer thrives when planning a multi-level system. Think of each tier as a unique micro-environment with specific light and moisture conditions. For the lower levels, shade-tolerant plants like ferns and hostas are ideal, as they flourish in the cooler, more protected spaces beneath taller structures. These plants add lush greenery and can help stabilize the soil, preventing erosion. On the upper tiers, sun-loving plants such as peppers, tomatoes, and sunflowers bask in the abundant light, growing tall and strong. The height and placement of each plant should be carefully considered to ensure that taller plants don't overshadow those that require more light.

Constructing a multi-level garden begins with understanding the lay of your land. If you're working with a slope, retaining walls can be your best friend. These walls support the soil and create flat areas where you can build your raised beds. Materials like stone, timber, or even recycled materials can be used to construct these walls, each offering a different aesthetic and structural quality.

Alternatively, pyramid structures are another creative option for compact spaces. By stacking layers of soil in a pyramid shape, you create a striking centerpiece that can hold a variety of plants. This approach maximizes vertical space and can be tailored to fit the exact dimensions of your garden.

While multi-level gardening systems offer many benefits, such as increased accessibility and a reduction in soil compaction, they also come with challenges. Water drainage can be tricky, as water tends to run downhill, potentially eroding soil and depriving upper levels of moisture. Consider installing a drip irrigation system that delivers water directly to each level to combat this. This helps with even distribution and reduces the risk of erosion. Additionally, incorporating organic matter or mulch can help retain moisture while stabilizing the soil. Another consideration is the potential for soil erosion, mainly if your garden is on a steep slope. Plant roots and retaining structures work together to hold the soil in place, but regular maintenance and monitoring are key to preventing any issues.

Multi-level raised bed systems bring a unique blend of functionality and beauty to your garden. They allow you to make the most of challenging terrain while creating a visually captivating landscape. Whether you're looking to improve access, increase planting space, or simply add an intriguing element to your garden, these systems offer a versatile solution. As you consider your options, consider how each level can complement the others, creating a cohesive and harmonious garden. With thoughtful planning and execution, your multi-level raised bed garden will become a thriving haven for plants and a delightful space for you to enjoy.

Chapter Four

Enhancing Garden Aesthetics

Picture yourself stepping into your garden, where every element—plants, pathways, and structures—melds seamlessly into a harmonious landscape. This is the magic of integrating raised beds into your existing garden layout, where the beds not only serve a functional purpose but also enhance the visual appeal of your outdoor space. It's about making your garden not just a place to grow food but a personal sanctuary.

Integrating raised beds into your landscape isn't just about plopping them down wherever there's space. It's about creating a cohesive garden design that feels intentional and well-planned. Start by considering the materials of your garden beds. If your home features wooden elements, like a deck or fencing, match your beds with similar wood to create a unified look. This consistency in materials ties your garden together, giving it a polished, professional feel. Alternatively, if your garden features modern elements like metal or glass, opt for metal raised beds that echo these materials, creating a sleek and contemporary vibe. Place your beds in harmony with natural sightlines, ensuring they guide the eye smoothly over the landscape.

Strategic layout planning is key to achieving a balanced and beautiful garden. The symmetrical placement of raised beds can create a sense of order and harmony, perfect for formal garden settings. Imagine a neatly arranged series of beds, each mirroring the other, forming a pleasing pattern that invites exploration. On the other hand, incorporating curves and angles can add a dynamic flow to your garden, ideal for a more relaxed, informal design. Curved pathways that wind through your raised beds create a sense of journey, encouraging you to discover what lies around each bend. Angles can be used to create visual interest, breaking up monotony and adding a touch of intrigue.

Complementary structures can further enhance the cohesion of your garden. Imagine adding a garden path that connects your raised beds, inviting you to stroll through your garden and enjoy its beauty from every angle. Paths can be made from gravel, stone, or even brick, each offering a different texture and feel. Consider incorporating arches or pergolas for vertical continuity. These structures provide support for climbing plants and frame your garden, creating a sense of enclosure and intimacy. The interplay of light and shadow as the sun filters through the pergola's beams adds an ever-changing dimension to your garden's aesthetics.

Of course, integrating raised beds into an existing landscape comes with its challenges. Still, with a bit of creativity, they can be overcome. Adjusting the height of your beds to match existing elements, like retaining walls or patio edges, ensures a seamless transition and avoids jarring visual breaks. This modification can be as simple as adding additional soil or using raised bed extenders to achieve the desired height. Managing transitions between different garden areas requires careful consideration of pathways and sight lines, ensuring each section of your garden flows naturally into the next. Use plants, garden art, or structures to soften and blur these boundaries, creating a unified and harmonious space.

Exercise: Visualize Your Garden

Take a moment to sit in your garden with a notepad. Sketch your existing landscape, noting key features like paths, structures, and focal points. Envision where raised beds could fit and how they might align with these elements. Consider materials, sight lines, and complementary structures. This exercise will help you visualize the potential of your garden and guide your integration efforts, ensuring your raised beds enhance the overall aesthetic.

Creative Edging and Decorative Elements

Imagine stepping into your garden and feeling an immediate sense of enchantment and beauty. This magic often starts with the subtle yet impactful use of edging and decorative elements. Edging is a versatile tool that helps define your garden beds' boundaries, adding structure and style. Natural stones make a wonderful choice if you're aiming for a rustic and earthy aesthetic. Their varied shapes and textures can transform the edges of your raised beds into a charming, organic feature. On the other hand, if your garden leans towards a more modern design, sleek metal or even durable plastic edging can provide clean lines that enhance the contemporary feel. These materials are practical in keeping soil neatly contained and elevate the overall look of your garden.

Decorative elements are where you can let your creativity shine, turning your garden into a personal expression of your style. Picture mosaic tiles embedded into your raised bed walls, each piece telling a story through its colorful patterns. Or consider painting stones with vibrant designs and scattering them throughout your garden. These small accents can create focal points that draw the eye and add a touch of whimsy. As dusk falls, imagine the soft glow of fairy lights or lanterns illuminating your pathways, casting a warm and inviting light that transforms your garden into an evening oasis. These lighting elements not only enhance ambiance but also extend the enjoyment of your garden into the night.

Personalizing your garden with handmade decorations can be incredibly rewarding if you're inclined towards DIY projects. Crafting wooden signs or plant labels is a simple yet effective way to add a personal touch. Use weatherproof paint to inscribe plant names, garden quotes, or even your own artistic designs. For a more tactile project, consider making stepping stones with embedded designs. Mix and pour concrete into molds, then press in colorful glass beads, pieces of tile, or even handprints for a truly unique path. These projects beautify your garden and provide a sense of accomplishment and connection to your space.

Color and texture are vital elements that can make or break your garden's aesthetic. Mixing different textures, such as the roughness of stone against the smoothness of metal, creates visual interest that keeps the eye engaged. When considering colors, think about the existing hues in your garden and choose schemes that harmonize with your plants. Complementary colors can create striking contrasts, while monochromatic palettes offer a more subtle and cohesive look. By carefully selecting and combining colors and textures, you can craft a garden that feels balanced and pleasing to both the eye and the soul.

Choosing Plant Varieties for Aesthetic Appeal

Selecting the right plant varieties is like curating an art collection. Each plant adds a unique texture, color, and form to your garden, contributing to its overall aesthetic appeal. Imagine a garden where every corner offers a different visual experience, from the soft rustle of ornamental grasses to the vibrant splash of blooming flowers. This diversity starts with the thoughtful choice of plants, incorporating a mix of foliage textures that can transform even the simplest garden into a visual masterpiece. Consider integrating plants with broad, glossy leaves alongside those with fine, feathery fronds. This contrast in textures creates depth and interest, drawing the eye and inviting exploration.

Creating a garden that captivates throughout the seasons requires selecting plants with varied bloom times. Picture a garden that offers a continuous parade of colors, from the early yellows of daffodils in spring to the deep purples of asters in fall. Choosing plants that bloom at different times guarantees that your garden remains lively and engaging year-round. This strategy not only enhances the aesthetic but also provides a dynamic landscape that evolves with the seasons. The anticipation of new blooms keeps the garden fresh and exciting, a living canvas that changes with the passing months.

Color schemes are another powerful tool in the gardener's palette. Developing cohesive and striking color palettes can transform your garden into a harmonious sanctuary or a vibrant explosion of hues. Complementary color schemes, like the pairing of blue and orange flowers, create a lively contrast that energizes the space. Alternatively, a monochromatic scheme, using variations of a single color, can evoke a sense of calm and unity. Seasonal color changes further add to the garden's vibrancy. Imagine the warm reds and golds of autumn leaves transitioning into the cool whites and blues of winter blooms. These shifts mark the passage of time and highlight the garden's adaptability and resilience.

Focal plants are the stars of your garden, drawing attention and adding drama. Tall, dramatic plants like sunflowers reach for the sky, creating vertical interest and serving as natural focal points. Ornamental grasses sway gently in the breeze, their movement adding a sense of life and vitality. Unique foliage plants, such as coleus with its intricate leaf patterns or hostas with their lush, layered leaves, offer visual anchors that ground the garden. These standout plants not only capture attention but also provide structure and shape, guiding the eye and creating a sense of order amidst the chaos of nature.

Incorporating pollinator-friendly plants not only enhances the beauty of your garden but also supports local ecosystems. Lavender and echinacea attract butterflies with their fragrant blooms and vibrant colors, creating a flutter of activity that adds an animated dimension to the garden. Bee balm and salvia are magnets for bees, and their nectar-rich flowers support these essential pollinators. By integrating these plants into your garden, you create a haven for beneficial insects, enhancing biodiversity and contributing to the health of your local environment. This approach enriches the aesthetic and aligns with sustainable gardening practices, promoting a balanced and thriving ecosystem.

The art of choosing plant varieties goes beyond mere aesthetics. It's about creating a garden that reflects your style, engages the senses, and supports the environment. By thoughtfully selecting plants for their textures, colors, and ecological benefits, you craft a space that is beautiful, functional, and alive. Each plant becomes a brushstroke in a larger picture, contributing to a garden that is as rewarding to cultivate as it is to behold.

Incorporating Art and Accessories into Your Garden

Garden art can add that extra layer of personality and style, making your garden not just a place to grow plants but a reflection of who you are. Sculptures and statues are excellent choices for adding focal points that draw the eye. Picture a graceful statue nestled among the flowers, its presence adding a touch of elegance and intrigue. Whether you choose abstract metal forms or classic stone figures, these pieces can anchor your garden, offering visual interest even when plants are out of bloom. For vertical intrigue, consider wall art or murals. These can transform a plain fence or wall into a canvas, bringing color and creativity to your garden. Murals depicting nature scenes or abstract designs can complement the plants around them, creating a cohesive look that ties your garden together.

Selecting the right garden accessories is about enhancing your space's beauty and functionality. Garden benches or seating areas invite you to linger and enjoy the fruits of your labor. Imagine a cozy nook with a weather-resistant bench where you can sip your morning coffee surrounded by the scent of blooming flowers. These seating areas can be crafted from wood, metal, or even recycled materials, each offering a different aesthetic. Birdbaths or feeders bring wildlife into your garden and add charm and movement. Watching birds flutter and splash adds a dynamic element to your garden, making it a lively and engaging space.

For those who enjoy a hands-on approach, DIY art projects can personalize your garden. Old pots or containers can be transformed with a splash of paint, turning them into colorful accents that brighten any corner. Consider painting them with patterns or motifs that resonate with your style. Another fun project is crafting wind chimes or mobiles from recycled materials. This can be as simple as stringing together old keys, beads, and shells. Hang them from a tree or pergola, and let the gentle tinkling sounds add a soothing soundtrack to your garden experience.

Lighting is the unsung hero of garden design, capable of transforming your space from day to night. Solar lights along pathways not only provide safety but also create a warm ambiance. Uplighting is another powerful tool used to accentuate architectural plants or structures. By placing lights at the base of trees or tall plants, you create dramatic shadows and highlights, adding depth and dimension to your garden. This interplay of light and shadow can turn your garden into a magical place where familiar plants take on new forms after dusk.

As you consider these artistic touches, think about how each element contributes to the garden's overall feel. It's about balance—choosing pieces that enhance rather than overwhelm, that invite exploration without dictating the experience. Your garden is a canvas, and these artistic elements are your palette. With a thoughtful approach, you can create a space that is uniquely yours, a place where art and nature come together to tell your story.

To wrap things up on garden design, incorporating art and accessories elevates your garden's aesthetics and enriches the overall experience, making it a place to relax, reflect, and find joy. This blend of creativity with functionality sets a vibrant scene, leading us to explore how these elements can harmonize with the broader garden environment.

Chapter Five

Soil Composition and Health

Ever wondered why some gardens flourish while others struggle to survive? The secret often lies beneath the surface—in the soil itself. Soil might seem like just dirt, but it's the lifeblood of any garden, especially when it comes to raised beds. Your plants depend on it for nutrients, water, and a solid foundation. Think of it as the stage on which your garden's performance unfolds. Great soil can be the difference between a bountiful harvest and a frustrating season of wilted leaves and stunted growth. In this chapter, we'll dig into the art of crafting the perfect soil mix, one that will set your raised bed garden up for success from the start.

Creating the Ideal Soil Mix for Raised Beds

The foundation of your raised bed garden lies in a well-balanced soil mix. The proper mix is very important as it provides both the structure and nutrients your plants need to thrive. The ideal blend consists of three main components: topsoil, compost, and perlite or vermiculite. Each plays a distinct role in creating an environment where plant roots can flourish. Topsoil forms the backbone of your mix, offering structure and volume. It's the canvas on which everything else is built. When selecting topsoil, look for a product that's dark, crumbly, and free of debris. Avoid soils with too much sand or clay, as these can lead to drainage issues or compaction.

Compost is the powerhouse of your soil mix. Rich in organic matter, it enhances nutrient supply and boosts microbial activity, which is critical for plant health. It breaks down slowly over time, releasing nutrients that feed your plants and improve soil structure. Compost also improves water retention, ensuring that your plants have access to moisture even during dry spells. Perlite or vermiculite, on the other hand, plays a vital role in aeration and drainage. These lightweight additives prevent soil compaction, allowing roots to penetrate easily and access the oxygen they need. They also help excess water drain away quickly, preventing root rot and other moisture-related issues.

Achieving the right soil mix proportions is key to creating a healthy environment for your plants. A commonly recommended ratio is 60% topsoil, 30% compost, and 10% perlite. Start by measuring out each component separately. Once you have your ingredients, it's time to mix them. Spread the materials on a tarp or wheelbarrow and combine them thoroughly with a shovel or rake. The goal is to achieve a homogeneous mixture with evenly distributed components. Take your time during this step—an even mix ensures that your plants will have consistent access to nutrients and good drainage throughout the bed.

Common mistakes in soil mixing can lead to problems down the road, but with a little foresight, they can be easily avoided. One frequent error is relying too heavily on one component, such as adding too much compost. While compost is beneficial, excessive amounts can lead to nutrient imbalances and poor drainage. Similarly, too little perlite can result in compacted soil, making it difficult for roots to grow. Striking the right balance helps your soil retain moisture while allowing excess water to escape, creating an ideal environment for plant growth.

Soil Mix Checklist

To help you stay on track, here's a quick checklist for creating your ideal soil mix:

- Measure and mix 60% topsoil, 30% compost, and 10% perlite.

- Choose topsoil that's dark, crumbly, and free of debris.

- Ensure compost is decomposed and free of contaminants.

- Mix ingredients thoroughly for even distribution.

- The mix should be light, airy, and free-draining.

With this guide, you're well on your way to creating a thriving raised bed garden. Your plants will thank you with lush growth and abundant harvests, all starting from the healthy soil beneath their roots.

Understanding Soil pH and Nutrient Balancing

Have you ever wondered why some plants thrive while others seem to struggle, even when they're side by side? One key factor is soil pH, a measure of acidity or alkalinity that can significantly impact plant health. This scale ranges from 0 to 14, with 7 being neutral. Most vegetables prefer a pH range between 6.0 and 7.0. This sweet spot is where nutrients are most readily available to plants, allowing them to absorb the essential elements they need for growth. Suppose the pH is too low (acidic) or too high (alkaline). In that case, nutrient uptake can be hindered, leaving plants unable to access the goodness in the soil. For instance, in overly acidic soil, phosphorus becomes less available, which can stunt plant growth. Conversely, an alkaline environment may cause iron and manganese deficiencies, leading to yellowing leaves and poor health.

Testing your soil's pH is a straightforward process that can save you headaches down the road. Home soil test kits are widely available and easy to use. Simply collect a soil sample from your raised bed, mix it with water, and apply the provided solution. The resulting color change will indicate your soil's pH level. If you find your soil is too acidic, lime is your go-to remedy. Lime, a natural mineral, gently raises pH levels, making the soil more alkaline. It's best applied in the fall, giving it time to alter the pH before spring planting. On the other hand, if your soil is too alkaline, sulfur can help lower the pH. Sulfur works more slowly than lime, but it's effective in making the soil more acidic, particularly when applied in warmer months when microbial activity can help speed up the process.

Balancing nutrients in your soil is equally important for a healthy garden. Essential nutrients include nitrogen, phosphorus, and potassium, often referred to as NPK. Nitrogen promotes lush, green growth, phosphorus supports root development and flowering, and potassium strengthens overall plant health. To keep these nutrients in balance, consider incorporating organic fertilizers like bone meal, which is rich in phosphorus, and blood meal which is high in nitrogen. Regularly monitoring your soil's nutrient levels is an important step in making sure your plants receive the balanced diet they need to flourish. A simple soil test can reveal any deficiencies, guiding your choice of amendments.

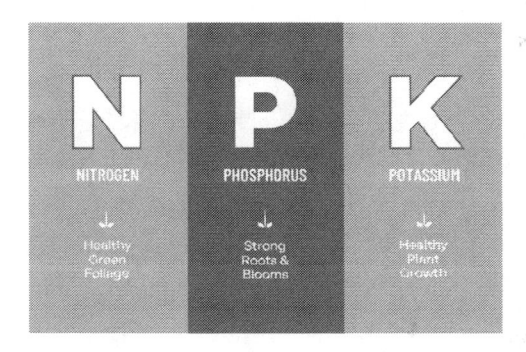

Identifying nutrient deficiencies can sometimes feel like solving a mystery, but plants often give clear clues. Yellowing leaves, for instance, frequently signal a lack of nitrogen. This nutrient is vital for the production of chlorophyll, the pigment responsible for photosynthesis. Without enough nitrogen, plants can't produce the energy they need, resulting in pale, weak growth. Adding a nitrogen-rich amendment like composted manure can quickly remedy this issue, restoring the vibrant green color to your plants. Stunted growth might point to a phosphorus shortage. Phosphorus is crucial for energy transfer in plants, affecting everything from root development to fruiting. If your plants seem small and underdeveloped, consider adding bone meal to boost phosphorus levels and encourage robust growth.

By understanding soil pH and nutrient balancing, you empower yourself to create an environment where your plants can thrive. The correct pH ensures nutrients are available, while balanced nutrition supports healthy growth and abundant harvests. With these insights, your raised bed garden is primed for success, nurturing plants that are beautiful and bountiful.

Organic Amendments to Boost Soil Fertility

When it comes to enriching your garden soil, organic amendments are like nature's gift to your plants. They boost fertility and improve the soil's texture and structure. Let's start with manure, a time-tested amendment known for its high nitrogen content. Nitrogen is key for leafy growth, making manure an excellent choice for supporting green, lush plants. Beyond nitrogen, manure adds organic matter that enhances soil structure, improving its ability to retain moisture and nutrients. However, using aged or composted manure is essential to avoid burning your plants with excess salts and ammonia. Fresh manure can be too potent, potentially harming delicate roots and introducing pathogens.

Green manure crops like clover offer a different approach to boosting soil fertility. These crops are grown specifically to be incorporated into the soil, breaking down and releasing nutrients. Clover, for example, is a fantastic nitrogen fixer. It works harmoniously with soil bacteria to capture atmospheric nitrogen, converting it into a form plants can use. This process enriches the soil without synthetic fertilizers, making it a sustainable choice for environmentally conscious gardeners. Once the clover has grown, you simply till it into the soil, allowing it to decompose and release its stored nutrients, preparing your beds for the next planting.

Worm castings are another gem in the world of organic amendments. These are essentially worm poop, and they pack a powerful punch for your plants. Full of beneficial microorganisms, worm castings enhance nutrient cycling, making nutrients more available to plants. They also improve soil structure and aeration, creating an environment where roots can breathe and water can flow freely. Incorporating worm castings into your soil mix or using them as a top dressing can improve plant health and vigor. Plus, they have the added benefit of suppressing certain soil-borne diseases, providing a natural defense for your garden. Worm castings, though beneficial, can be costly for large-scale applications. To manage costs, consider using them strategically as a supplement rather than a primary amendment.

Applying these amendments involves timing and technique. For maximum impact, incorporate them during soil preparation, mixing them thoroughly into the topsoil before planting. This ensures that the nutrients are readily available to seedlings as they establish themselves. Mid-season, you can boost your plants' growth by top-dressing with compost or worm castings. Simply spread a layer around the base of your plants, gently working it into the surface soil. This practice replenishes nutrients and stimulates microbial activity, supporting robust growth throughout the growing season.

While organic amendments offer numerous benefits, they come with their own set of challenges. Over-application of manure, for instance, can lead to nutrient leaching, where excess nutrients wash away, polluting nearby waterways. To avoid this, apply manure in moderation and make sure that it's well-aged. Green manure crops can sometimes harbor weed seeds, which might sprout alongside your desired plants. To mitigate this, mow or till green manure before it sets seed, preventing unwanted growth.

By balancing the use of these organic amendments and being mindful of their potential drawbacks, you can create a vibrant, healthy environment for your plants. Your raised bed garden will thrive with the help of these natural enhancers, producing bountiful harvests that reflect the care and attention you've invested.

Maintaining Soil Health through Crop Rotation

Crop rotation, a practice rooted in ancient agriculture, is a cornerstone of sustainable gardening. It's a simple yet powerful way to maintain soil health and boost productivity in your raised beds. At its core, crop rotation involves alternating the types of crops you plant in a specific area each season. This method helps prevent the depletion of soil nutrients, as different plants have varying nutrient needs. For instance, leafy greens like lettuce and spinach often require abundant nitrogen. At the same time, root crops such as carrots and beets might demand more potassium. By rotating these crops, the soil can replenish naturally, maintaining a balanced nutrient profile without relying heavily on fertilizers.

Beyond nutrient management, crop rotation is instrumental in disrupting the cycles of pests and diseases. Many garden pests and pathogens are crop-specific, thriving on the same plants year after year. By changing your plantings, you deny these unwanted guests a continuous food source, effectively breaking their life cycle. This results in fewer infestations and diseases, reducing the need for chemical interventions. Imagine the relief of knowing that your tomatoes won't fall prey to the same blight that troubled them last season simply because you've rotated them out of their usual spot.

Planning effective rotation cycles requires a bit of strategy but can be straightforward once you get the hang of it. Start by grouping your plants by family, such as legumes, nightshades, and brassicas. Each family has similar nutrient demands and pest susceptibilities. By rotating these groups, you verify that no single family depletes the soil or attracts pests over successive seasons. A multi-year rotation schedule can help you keep track of what was planted, where, and when, making it easier to plan your future crops. For example, after growing nitrogen-fixing legumes like beans in one bed, you might follow with heavy feeders such as tomatoes, which will benefit from the residual nitrogen left in the soil. Another strategy involves rotating root crops with leafy greens. Root crops can help break up the soil, improving its structure for the next planting. By following root crops with shallow-rooted leafy greens, you maximize the use of the entire soil profile, ensuring that no space goes to waste.

However, crop rotation has challenges, especially if you're working with limited space. Strategic rotation becomes essential when every square foot counts. One solution is to incorporate container gardening as part of your rotation plan. Containers offer the flexibility to move crops around, effectively expanding your available planting area. This allows you to maintain rotation principles even in a compact garden. Additionally, adapting your rotation plans to fit personal gardening goals is essential. Maybe you're focused on growing a particular vegetable for a special recipe or aiming to experiment with new varieties. In such cases, consider minor adjustments to your rotation schedule to accommodate these goals without sacrificing soil health.

In summary, crop rotation in raised bed gardening is about smart, intentional planting that benefits both the garden and the gardener. It keeps soil nutrients balanced, disrupts pest cycles, and encourages a diverse planting scheme that continually renews itself. By implementing thoughtful rotation plans, you can enjoy healthier plants, reduced pest issues, and more robust harvests. As you plan your next planting season, remember that variety isn't just the spice of life—it's the key to a thriving garden.

Chapter Six

Watering Systems and Techniques

Have you ever watched rain gently fall on your garden and wondered how to replicate that perfect, even watering? Well, drip irrigation might just be the answer you're looking for. It's like having a personal raincloud that delivers water right where your plants need it most—at the roots. This method is efficient and environmentally friendly, making it a favorite among gardeners striving for sustainability. By minimizing water waste and targeting irrigation precisely, drip systems offer a modern solution that benefits both your plants and the planet.

Drip irrigation is all about precision. It delivers water directly to the root zone, which means your plants get exactly what they need without the excess. This targeted approach reduces water evaporation and runoff, ensuring that every drop counts. Less water on the leaves also means fewer opportunities for fungal diseases, which thrive in damp environments. In addition, by watering only where your plants are growing, you discourage weeds from sprouting in the surrounding soil. The result? A healthier garden with minimal maintenance.

Setting up a drip irrigation system might seem daunting at first, but once you break it down, it's quite manageable. The key components include drip lines, emitters, filters, and pressure regulators. Drip lines are the veins of your system, carrying water from the source to your plants. Emitters are spaced along these lines, slowly releasing water directly into the soil. Filters are crucial for preventing clogs and ensuring that your system runs smoothly. Without a filter, small particles can block the emitters, disrupting water flow. Pressure regulators maintain a consistent water flow, adjusting for any changes in pressure. This helps with uniform watering across your entire garden, no matter its size.

When you're ready to install your system, start by planning your irrigation layout. Consider the placement of your beds and the specific water needs of different plants. Draw a simple map to visualize where the drip lines and emitters will go. Lay out your hoses and connect them to the water source, making sure to include your filters and pressure regulators. Place emitters strategically, spacing them to cover the entire root zone of each plant. Once everything is in position, test the system for leaks and ensure that water is reaching all areas evenly. Adjust as needed to optimize coverage and efficiency.

Maintaining your drip irrigation system is straightforward but essential for long-term success. Regularly check and clean the filters and emitters to prevent clogs. Over time, mineral deposits and debris can accumulate, so a periodic clean-up keeps the water flowing freely. Adjust the system seasonally to accommodate changing water needs. Your plants may require more frequent watering in the hotter months, while cooler seasons might demand less. By staying on top of these adjustments, you are helping your garden to remain healthy and well-hydrated throughout the year.

Quick Checklist: Drip Irrigation Installation

- Plan your layout by mapping out beds and water needs.

- Install drip lines, ensuring emitter placement covers the root zones.

- Connect filters to prevent clogs and pressure regulators for consistent flow.

- Test for leaks and adjust emitter spacing for optimal coverage.

- Schedule regular maintenance to clean filters and adjust seasonal flow.

With these steps, you'll have a drip irrigation system that transforms your raised bed garden into a thriving oasis, providing the perfect moisture balance for robust plant growth.

Building Self-Watering Wicking Beds

Imagine your garden thriving with minimal effort on your part. That's the magic of wicking beds, a clever self-watering system that consistently supplies moisture to your plants. These beds operate on the principle of capillary action, drawing water upward from a reservoir below. This passive delivery system gives your plants a steady moisture supply, reducing the need for manual watering. It's a game-changer, especially for those of us who can't always be on hand to water daily.

With wicking beds, your plants benefit from enhanced root growth, as the consistent moisture encourages roots to grow deep and strong, reaching down to the water source.

To build a wicking bed, you must select an appropriate container or construct a bed. Start by choosing a sturdy container with a depth of at least 16 inches. Many gardeners opt for recycled containers, which are environmentally friendly and cost-effective. Once you've selected your container, installing a water reservoir at the base is next. This reservoir can be created using perforated pipes or a shallow tray that allows water to pool at the bottom. The key is to maintain a balance where the reservoir holds enough water for consistent wicking but isn't so deep that it drowns the roots.

After setting up the reservoir, you'll need to add a wicking medium that draws moisture from the reservoir up into the soil. Common materials for this layer include a mix of peat moss, vermiculite, and perlite. These materials are effective because they wick water efficiently and provide good aeration for the roots. Spread this medium evenly across the reservoir, ensuring it makes contact with both the water source and the soil above. This connection is necessary for the capillary action to work, allowing water to move upward to where the roots can access it.

When it comes to materials and design, you have several options. Recycled containers, as mentioned, are a sustainable choice, but you can also use wood, stone, or even metal to construct your wicking beds. Just make sure the materials are safe for growing food and won't leach harmful chemicals into the soil. Incorporating overflow outlets is another important step. These outlets allow excess water to escape, preventing overwatering and ensuring your plants aren't sitting in soggy conditions. They also help maintain the optimal water level within the reservoir, contributing to the system's efficiency.

Wicking beds come with challenges, but they can be easily managed with a bit of foresight. Algae growth in the water reservoir can become an issue if the area is exposed to sunlight. To combat this, consider covering the reservoir with a light-blocking material or placing a lid over it. This simple measure can prevent sunlight from reaching the water, inhibiting algae growth. Another potential challenge is ensuring the wicking medium performs optimally. If you notice uneven water distribution, it might be necessary to adjust the composition of your wicking medium or check for blockages that might impede capillary action. Regularly maintaining the system by checking for such issues will guarantee it functions smoothly and effectively.

Water Conservation Techniques for Drought-Prone Areas

In regions where every drop of water is precious, the importance of water conservation in gardening cannot be overstated. Drought-prone areas present a unique challenge to gardeners, insisting on innovative strategies to ensure plant survival while adhering to water restrictions. It's all about finding ways to nurture your garden without overusing this limited resource. Reducing overall water usage not only supports the health of your plants but also contributes to a more sustainable environment. The key is to make every drop count, ensuring that water reaches your plants effectively and efficiently.

Mulching is a fantastic method to help retain moisture in the soil, acting as a protective blanket that shields it from the harsh sun. Organic mulches like straw or wood chips are excellent choices. They decompose over time, enriching the soil with nutrients while keeping it cool and moist.

These mulches reduce evaporation, meaning the water you give your plants stays in the soil longer. Another option is reflective mulches, designed to reduce soil temperature by reflecting sunlight. These are particularly useful in hot climates where soil can quickly overheat, leading to water loss and plant stress. By maintaining a stable soil temperature, these mulches help your garden conserve water and thrive even in less-than-ideal conditions.

Exploring alternative watering techniques can also greatly enhance your water conservation efforts. One method gaining popularity is using grey water for irrigation. Grey water systems recycle water from household activities like laundry and dish washing, redirecting it to your garden instead of letting it go to waste. While not suitable for every plant type, many ornamentals and non-edible plants can benefit from this practice, reducing your reliance on fresh water.

Another effective approach is rainwater harvesting. Collecting rainwater from rooftops and storing it in barrels or tanks creates a reserve that can be used during dry spells. This not only eases the pressure on municipal water supplies but also provides your garden with a natural, untreated water source that's free from the chemicals often found in city tap water.

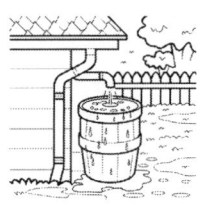

Optimizing water usage doesn't have to be complicated. Simple strategies can make a big difference. For instance, watering during the cooler parts of the day—early morning or late evening—reduces evaporation as the sun is less intense. This gives the plants time to absorb water before the heat of the day sets in. Grouping plants with similar water needs together is another smart tactic. By placing thirstier plants in one area and drought-tolerant varieties in another, you can tailor your watering schedule more precisely, ensuring each plant gets the right amount of water without waste. This strategic planting method conserves water and promotes healthier plant growth by reducing competition for resources.

Water Conservation Tips: Quick Reference

- Use organic mulches to retain soil moisture and reduce evaporation.

- Consider reflective mulches for hot climates to keep soil temperatures down.

- Recycle household grey water for irrigation when appropriate.

- Install rainwater harvesting systems to collect and store natural water.

- Water during cooler hours to minimize evaporation.

- Group plants by water need to optimize watering efficiency.

Incorporating these techniques into your gardening routine helps create a resilient garden capable of withstanding the challenges of drought conditions. By embracing these practices, you support both your plants and the environment, ensuring that your garden remains a vibrant, sustainable oasis.

Troubleshooting Common Watering Issues

Watering might seem straightforward, but any seasoned gardener will tell you that it can be a bit of a balancing act. Too much water, and you risk drowning your plants, leading to soggy roots and yellowing leaves—a classic sign of over watering. On the flip side, too little water results in wilting and dry soil, leaving your plants thirsty and struggling. Recognizing these symptoms is the first step in correcting your watering woes, and fortunately, there are practical solutions to help you strike that perfect moisture balance.

Adjusting your watering frequency and depth is crucial when you notice signs of stress in your plants. If over watering is the culprit, it's time to ease up on the hose. Allow the soil to dry out between waterings, which encourages roots to grow deeper, seeking out moisture. This not only strengthens the plants but also helps prevent root rot. Improving drainage in waterlogged beds is essential. Consider adding organic matter like compost to the soil, which enhances its structure and allows excess water to escape. For those with persistent issues, raised beds can be a lifesaver, naturally promoting better drainage due to their elevation.

Tools for monitoring soil moisture can be incredibly helpful, providing insights that aren't always visible to the naked eye. Moisture meters are a gardener's best friend, offering precise readings of how much water is present in the soil. Simply insert the probe into the soil, and the meter will give you an immediate snapshot of moisture levels. For a low-tech alternative, the finger test is a tried-and-true method. Stick your finger into the soil up to the second knuckle. If the soil feels dry at that depth, it's time to water. If it feels moist, hold off for a bit. This simple technique allows you to gauge how much water your plants truly need without over-relying on external tools.

Creating a watering schedule tailored to your garden's specific needs is the final piece of the puzzle. Start by considering seasonal variations. Plants typically need more water during the hot summer months, while less frequent watering might suffice in cooler seasons. Climate conditions in your area will also influence how often you need to water, so keep an eye on the weather forecast. Additionally, adapting your schedule based on plant growth stages can optimize water usage. Newly planted seedlings may require gentle, more frequent watering, while established plants can handle deeper, less frequent soaks that encourage robust root development.

As you refine your watering practices, remember that flexibility is key. No two gardens are alike, and factors like soil type, plant variety, and micro-climates can all influence how much water your garden needs. By staying observant and responsive, you can develop a watering routine that supports healthy growth and abundant harvests, all while conserving this precious resource.

Share the Gift of Growth

Did you know that sharing your experience can inspire others to grow their own gardens? It's true! When you leave a review, you help someone just like you—someone excited about gardening but not sure how to start.

My goal is to make raised bed gardening simple, enjoyable, and accessible to everyone. With your help, we can encourage more people to dig in and discover the joy of growing their own food.

Most people decide which books to read based on reviews. That's why I'm asking for your support. Leaving a review takes less than a minute, costs nothing, and can make a world of difference. Your feedback might inspire:

- A first-time gardener to start their journey.

- A family to grow fresh, healthy food in their backyard.

- A community to come together through gardening.

- A dream of a thriving, sustainable garden to come true.

To make an impact, please consider leaving this book a review on Amazon!

Chapter Seven

Companion Planting and Crop Rotation

Imagine your garden as a thriving community where each plant has a role to play, interacting with its neighbors to create a harmonious ecosystem. This is the essence of companion planting—a practice that involves strategically pairing plants to enhance growth, flavor, and pest control. It's like setting the perfect dinner party where guests complement each other, resulting in a more enjoyable experience for everyone. Companion planting is about growing plants together and understanding the complex web of ecological interactions that can transform your raised bed garden into a vibrant and balanced ecosystem.

One fascinating aspect of companion planting is allelopathy, where certain plants release chemicals that can inhibit or promote the growth of nearby plants. While this might sound like plant warfare, it's a natural mechanism some plants use to create a more favorable growing environment. For instance, walnut trees are known for their allelopathic properties, producing a chemical called juglone that can stunt the growth of certain sensitive plants. Conversely, some plants release substances that stimulate growth or repel pests, creating a protective barrier for their companions.

Symbiotic relationships are another cornerstone of companion planting. These mutual benefits often involve nitrogen-fixing legumes like beans and peas, which form partnerships with soil bacteria to capture atmospheric nitrogen and convert it into a form plants can use. This natural fertilizer enriches the soil, benefiting the legumes and neighboring plants that tap into this nutrient-rich environment. By planting nitrogen-fixers alongside heavy feeders like corn, you create a dynamic system where each plant contributes to the health and productivity of the garden.

Biodiversity is the unsung hero of companion planting. A diverse garden teems with life, attracting pollinators like bees and butterflies that flit from flower to flower, ensuring a bountiful harvest. Diverse flowering plants draw in these essential pollinators, boosting fruit set and leading to more productive crops. Moreover, biodiversity enhances resilience against pests and diseases, as monocultures (single-species plantings) are more susceptible to outbreaks. A garden filled with various plants confuses pests, making it harder for them to locate their preferred hosts while attracting beneficial insects that keep pest populations in check.

Successful plant pairings are the heart of companion planting. Take, for instance, the classic duo of basil and tomatoes. Not only does basil enhance the flavor of tomatoes, but it also acts as a natural pest deterrent, keeping aphids and tomato hornworms at bay. This flavorful partnership results in tastier tomatoes and a healthier garden. Similarly, carrots and onions make an excellent pair. Carrots can repel the carrot fly, while onions deter onion flies. By understanding these beneficial relationships, you can design a garden where plants support and protect each other.

Of course, companion planting presents its own set of challenges. One common issue is resource competition, where plants with similar needs vie for nutrients, water, or light. To avoid this, it's important to pair plants with complementary growth habits and requirements. For example, planting shade-tolerant crops under taller plants can maximize light use without causing competition. Varying light and water needs can also complicate companion planting efforts. When planning your garden, consider the specific needs of each plant, ensuring they receive adequate light, water, and nutrients without overshadowing or overburdening their companions.

QUICK REFLECTION: COMPANION PLANTING JOURNAL

Take a moment to jot down your observations in a journal. Note any successful plant pairings you've tried and their outcomes. Reflect on any challenges or surprises you encountered. This practice helps you learn from experience and guides future planting decisions, making your garden more efficient and productive.

Creating a Companion Planting Chart for Your Garden

Creating a companion planting chart is like crafting a personalized map for your garden. It begins with understanding your garden's unique goals and needs. Are you aiming for a bountiful harvest of fresh vegetables or a garden doubling as a pollinator haven? Identifying your key objectives helps guide your plant choices. Once you've outlined your goals, the next step is to identify the key crops you want to grow.

Consider the staples in your kitchen or the herbs you frequently use. After selecting these main crops, research their ideal companions using the guide on page 125. Don't shy away from exploring new pairings or experimenting with traditional ones that have proven successful over time.

Organizing your chart is necessary for clarity and usability. A well-designed chart not only makes the planting process smoother but also helps when you need to reference it quickly throughout the growing season.

Regarding specific recommendations, some plant pairings stand out for their effectiveness. For instance, tomatoes benefit significantly from being planted alongside marigolds. These vibrant flowers add a splash of color and deter nematodes, protecting your tomatoes from these pesky root invaders. Cucumbers, on the other hand, thrive when paired with radishes. Radishes can act as a trap crop, drawing pests away from your cucumbers and allowing them to grow unimpeded. Such pairings enhance your garden's productivity and health, making the time spent on your chart well worth the effort.

As you use your companion planting chart, remember that it's a living document. Your garden isn't static, and neither should your chart be. Throughout the growing season, be prepared to make seasonal adjustments. Some plants may thrive in cooler weather, while others prefer the warmth of summer. Update your chart to reflect these changes, ensuring that you're always planting the proper companions at the right time. Don't hesitate to integrate new plant varieties as you discover them. A new herb or vegetable can open up exciting possibilities for companion planting, keeping your garden fresh and dynamic.

EXERCISE: PERSONALIZE YOUR COMPANION PLANTING CHART

Study the companion planting guide on page 125 of this book and start pairing ideal plants together on a piece of paper. Refer back to your chart regularly, tweaking it as needed based on your observations and experiences. This exercise will help you visualize the relationships between plants, guide your choices, and make your garden planning more efficient and rewarding. Utilize the blank pages following the guide to take notes on your companion planting journey.

Implementing Crop Rotation for Healthier Soil

Crop rotation is a time-honored gardening practice that plays a vital role in maintaining soil health and ensuring a productive garden. By regularly changing the location of crops, you minimize the depletion of essential nutrients in the soil. Different plants have varying nutrient needs, and some are more demanding than others. For example, leafy greens and fruiting vegetables like tomatoes and peppers are heavy feeders, drawing significant nutrients from the soil. Without rotation, these plants can leave the soil exhausted and less fertile for subsequent plantings. Rotation helps balance these demands by following heavy feeders with crops that replenish the soil, like legumes, which fix nitrogen back into the earth. This method keeps your soil rich and balanced, reducing the need for additional fertilizers.

Another critical aspect of crop rotation is its ability to disrupt pest and disease cycles. Many pests and diseases are host-specific, thriving on particular plants and their relatives. When the same type of plant is grown in the same spot year after year, it gives these pests and diseases a consistent food source, leading to a buildup that can devastate crops. By rotating crops, you break this cycle, reducing the likelihood of infestations and infections. This simple shift can significantly diminish your garden's pest and disease pressures, allowing plants to thrive without chemical interventions. It's a natural way to maintain a healthier garden ecosystem.

Planning an effective crop rotation scheme requires a bit of forethought but is well worth the effort. Start by grouping your plants into families, such as nightshades, legumes, and brassicas. Each family has similar nutritional needs and pest vulnerabilities. By rotating these groups, you ensure that the soil is not continuously drained of the same nutrients and that pests have fewer opportunities to establish themselves. Designing a multi-year rotation plan will help you track what was planted, where, and when. A simple four-year rotation might involve moving each plant family to a new bed every year, allowing time for the soil to recover and pests to disperse.

Implementing crop rotation can seem daunting for gardeners working with limited space, but creative solutions exist. One approach is to use vertical growth to expand planting options. By training climbing plants like beans and cucumbers to grow upwards, you free up ground space for rotating other crops. This technique maximizes your available area and allows you to maintain rotation principles even in small gardens. Incorporating container gardening is another effective strategy. Containers are portable, making moving crops around easy and adhering to rotation plans. This flexibility helps prevent soil depletion and pest buildup, ensuring your garden remains healthy and productive.

Specific rotation cycles can guide you in planning your garden's layout. For instance, alternating root crops, fruiting crops, and leafy greens in successive seasons can keep your soil balanced and fertile. Root crops like carrots and beets can break up the soil, improving its structure and preparing it for the next planting. Fruiting crops, such as tomatoes and peppers, can follow, taking advantage of the improved soil conditions. Leafy greens, which are generally less demanding, can round off the cycle, utilizing the remaining nutrients and leaving the soil refreshed. Incorporating green manure crops, like clover or vetch, into your rotation can further rejuvenate the soil. These crops are grown and then tilled back into the soil, adding organic matter and boosting fertility. They act as a natural fertilizer, providing your garden with a nutrient boost without the need for synthetic inputs. This practice enhances soil health and supports sustainable gardening by reducing reliance on external fertilizers.

Pairing Plants for Natural Pest Control

Imagine your garden as a team, each plant playing its part to ward off unwanted pests. In this lineup, certain combinations shine at keeping those pesky intruders at bay. One of the standout pairings is garlic with roses. This might seem like an unusual duo, but they complement each other beautifully. Garlic releases sulfur compounds that aphids and other soft-bodied insects detest. When planted around roses, garlic acts as a natural shield, helping to protect those delicate blooms from aphid attacks. It's a simple yet effective strategy that can save you from using chemical pesticides.

Another favorite in the garden's defense lineup is nasturtiums. These vibrant, sprawling plants are more than just pretty faces; they are a trap crop for aphids and whiteflies. Nasturtiums attract these pests, luring them away from your prized vegetables. Picture them as decoys, sacrificing themselves so your main crops can thrive. Their bright flowers also attract beneficial insects, adding another layer of protection to your garden ecosystem. Planting nasturtiums around the perimeter of your garden or interspersed among your vegetables can create a protective barrier that keeps your plants safe and healthy.

Aromatic herbs also play a vital role in natural pest management. Lavender and sage are two herbs that bring delightful scents to your garden and ward off unwanted visitors like moths and beetles. The intense aromas of these herbs confuse pests, making it harder for them to locate their target plants. Planting lavender and sage near crops prone to pest attacks can add a fragrant layer of defense. These herbs are also versatile and can be used in cooking or for aromatic purposes, making them a valuable addition to any garden.

Strategic placement is key when integrating these pest-deterring pairs into your garden. Consider the vulnerability of your crops and arrange these protective plants accordingly. For instance, placing garlic and nasturtiums around the edges of your garden can form a natural barrier that pests must overcome to reach your vegetables. This perimeter planting not only enhances the visual appeal of your garden but also strengthens its defenses. You can also plant these companions in clusters around particularly susceptible plants, offering targeted protection where it's needed most.

However, it's essential to understand the limitations of using plant pairings for pest control. While these natural methods can significantly reduce pest populations, they might not eliminate them entirely. It's essential to recognize that plant-based deterrents are part of a broader pest management strategy. Complementing them with other organic techniques, such as handpicking pests or using natural sprays, can enhance their effectiveness. These methods work best as part of an integrated approach, combining the strengths of each to protect your garden from all angles.

In the end, pairing plants for natural pest control is a practical and sustainable way to safeguard your garden. By choosing the right combinations and strategically placing them, you create a resilient ecosystem that supports plant health and reduces reliance on chemical interventions. This approach benefits your garden and promotes a healthier environment, aligning with the broader goals of sustainable gardening. As you explore these plant pairings, you'll find that your garden becomes not just a place of growth but a thriving community where each plant contributes to the whole.

Chapter Eight

Natural Pest and Disease Management

Have you ever strolled through your garden only to spot a leaf curled in distress or a plant teeming with tiny intruders? It's a scene no gardener wants to encounter, yet understanding the common pests that plague raised beds is fundamental. These pests are like uninvited guests at a dinner party, and knowing how to identify them early can save your plants and sanity. Raised beds offer unique opportunities for pest control thanks to their structure and manageability. They allow you to easily implement strategies that keep the ecosystem in balance without resorting to harsh chemicals.

One frequent offender in raised bed gardens is the aphid. These small, sap-sucking insects are often found congregating on the undersides of leaves, feasting on your plants' vitality. Aphids come in various colors, including green, black, and even pink, making them sometimes hard to spot until the damage is done. They pierce plant tissues to suck out sap, leading to curled and yellowed leaves. This damage not only weakens the plant but also creates openings for disease. Slugs and snails are another common foe, especially after rain or during cool, damp nights. These mollusks leave behind a telltale trail of slime and large, irregular holes in foliage as they feast on tender leaves. If you notice these signs, it's time to take action before they devour your garden. Lastly, cabbage worms—those small, green larvae—are notorious for their appetite for brassicas like cabbage and broccoli. They chew through leaves, leaving behind ragged holes, and, if unchecked, can strip plants bare.

Recognizing pest damage early is key to maintaining a healthy garden. Leaf curling and yellowing are often the first signs of an aphid infestation. Inspect the undersides of leaves where aphids congregate, and look for sticky honeydew, a sugary substance they excrete, which can attract ants and lead to sooty mold. For slugs and snails, check for their silvery trails and the characteristic holes they create. These trails can often be found in the morning, glistening in the early light. Cabbage worms, with their voracious appetites, leave behind distinct feeding patterns. Examine the leaves of your brassicas carefully, especially the undersides, for these green caterpillars and their frass (insect poop), which looks like small, dark pellets.

Scouting your garden regularly for these signs can help catch problems before they become unmanageable. Make it a habit to inspect leaves and stems at least once a week, paying special attention to the undersides where pests often hide. Yellow sticky traps can be a valuable tool for monitoring flying insects like aphids and whiteflies. Place these traps near affected plants to capture pests on contact, giving you a clear indication of the pest pressure in your garden. This proactive approach helps manage current infestations and informs you when to take preventive measures.

Understanding the life cycles of common pests enables you to plan more effective control strategies. Many pests, such as beetles, undergo complete metamorphosis, passing through egg, larva, pupa, and adult stages. Knowing this sequence allows you to target vulnerable stages, such as larvae, which are often easier to control than adults. For instance, introducing beneficial nematodes can effectively target soil-dwelling pest larvae without harming plants or beneficial insects. Similarly, knowing when adult beetles are laying eggs can help you time your interventions, such as applying diatomaceous earth to deter newly hatched larvae. By tailoring your approach to each pest's life cycle, you can reduce their impact and keep your garden healthy.

Pest Identification Exercise

Create a pest journal to help you become more familiar with the pests in your garden. Document the pests you encounter, noting their appearance, the damage they cause, and any life cycle information you observe. Include sketches or photographs for reference. Over time, this journal will become a valuable resource, helping you quickly identify and manage pests before they can harm your garden.

Homemade Remedies for Pest Control

Gardening in raised beds can feel like a constant battle against pests, but before you reach for chemical sprays, consider the arsenal of natural solutions you probably already have at home. These homemade remedies protect your plants and maintain the health of your garden's ecosystem. One such remedy is a garlic and chili spray, a potent mix that deters a wide array of insects. Garlic, with its intense aroma, confuses pests. At the same time, the capsaicin in chili peppers acts as an irritant, keeping insects at bay. It's a simple concoction yet surprisingly effective at keeping unwanted critters off your plants.

To whip up this powerful spray, combine a few cloves of garlic with two or three hot chili peppers and a couple of cups of water. Let this mixture sit overnight, allowing the flavors to meld and intensify. The next day, strain the liquid into a spray bottle, adding a bit more water to dilute it. A drop or two of dish soap can help the solution adhere to plant leaves, increasing its effectiveness. Apply this spray to your plants in the early morning or late afternoon, avoiding the midday sun to prevent leaf burn. A word of caution: this mixture can irritate your skin, so it's wise to wear gloves during application.

Neem oil, another staple in organic gardening, serves as a natural insecticide with a track record for tackling garden pests. Derived from the seeds of the neem tree, this oil contains azadirachtin, a compound that disrupts the life cycle of many insects, including aphids, spider mites, and whiteflies. What's great about neem oil is its targeted approach—it affects pests without harming beneficial insects like ladybugs and bees when applied correctly. To create a neem oil solution, mix one to two tablespoons of neem oil with a gallon of water and a teaspoon of mild dish detergent. Shake well and use a spray bottle to apply the mixture to all surfaces of your plants. Like the garlic-chili spray, apply neem oil during cooler parts of the day.

The effectiveness of these natural remedies largely depends on consistency and timing. Unlike chemical pesticides that can offer a quick fix, natural solutions require regular application to maintain their impact. Plan to reapply your chosen treatment weekly, especially during peak pest seasons or after heavy rains, which can wash away the spray. While these remedies are generally safe for plants and beneficial insects, they do have their limitations. Persistent pests may require multiple treatments, and some insects might develop resistance over time, making it necessary to monitor your garden and adjust your strategies as needed.

Incorporating these remedies into your gardening routine can feel seamless with a bit of planning. Consider setting a specific day each week for pest control to verify it's done regularly. It is helpful to combine these sprays with other organic methods, like companion planting or introducing beneficial insects, for a holistic approach to pest management. For instance, planting marigolds alongside your vegetables can naturally deter nematodes, while releasing ladybugs in your garden can help control aphid populations. These practices not only support a balanced ecosystem but also empower you to manage pests sustainably.

DIY Pest Control Checklist

Create a checklist to track your pest management efforts. Note the recipes for each spray, their application frequency, and the pests they target. Record any changes in pest activity, and adjust your strategies as needed. Keep this checklist handy in your garden journal for easy reference and to refine your approach over time. This record-keeping not only helps you stay organized but also aids in understanding which methods work best for your specific garden conditions.

Disease Prevention and Treatment in Raised Beds

As you nurture your garden, diseases can be as unwelcome as a surprise frost. They often strike quietly, marring your plants with spots and wilts that hint at deeper issues. Powdery mildew is a common adversary, leaving behind a white, powdery residue on leaves. This fungal disease thrives in warm, dry conditions and can spread rapidly if not addressed. You'll recognize it by its dusty appearance, which can hinder photosynthesis and weaken plants over time. Another frequent visitor to your tomato and potato plants is blight. This disease manifests as dark, water-soaked spots on leaves and stems, eventually leading to wilting and plant death if left unchecked. Both these diseases challenge your gardening efforts, but with a bit of foresight and care, they can be managed effectively.

Preventing disease in your raised beds starts with cultural practices that create an environment where pathogens find it hard to thrive. Proper air circulation is a cornerstone of disease prevention. When plants are spaced appropriately, air flows freely between them, reducing humidity levels that fungi love. Crowded plants trap moisture, creating a breeding ground for mildew and blight. By giving each plant room to breathe, you're not just preventing disease but encouraging healthier growth overall. Another key practice is crop rotation. By changing the location of your crops each season, you minimize the risk of disease buildup in the soil. This is because many pathogens are crop-specific and can persist in the soil, waiting for their host plants to return. Rotating crops disrupts this cycle, offering a simple yet effective defense against recurring diseases.

When disease does rear its ugly head, organic treatment options provide a gentle yet effective solution. For powdery mildew, a baking soda spray can work wonders. Baking soda raises the pH on leaf surfaces, creating an environment that fungi find inhospitable. To make this spray, mix one tablespoon of baking soda with a gallon of water and a teaspoon of liquid soap. Apply it weekly to affected plants, ensuring coverage on both sides of the leaves. For blight, copper fungicides offer a natural option. Copper helps prevent the spread of fungal spores and can be applied as a preventive measure or at the first sign of disease. When using copper, follow label instructions carefully to avoid excessive buildup in the soil, which can harm beneficial organisms.

Keeping records of your garden's health can be a game changer in managing diseases. A garden journal serves as a valuable tool, allowing you to track conditions and outcomes over time. Record what you observe—whether it's sudden leaf spots or subtle color changes. Note the weather patterns leading up to these events, as humidity and temperature shifts often affect disease development. By documenting these details, you gain insights into recurring issues and can adjust your practices accordingly. This proactive approach helps you spot patterns and anticipate problems before they become widespread.

DISEASE MANAGEMENT EXERCISE

Create a disease management chart for your raised beds. List common diseases, their symptoms, and potential treatments. Record observations from your garden, noting which treatments work best. Over time, your chart will become a personalized guide, helping you make informed decisions and keep your garden thriving.

Understanding the nuances of disease prevention and treatment equips you with the skills to maintain a vibrant, healthy garden. Combining cultural practices with organic treatments and diligent record-keeping creates a resilient environment where your plants can flourish.

Encouraging Beneficial Insects and Wildlife

In the intricate dance of your garden, beneficial insects play a starring role in maintaining harmony. These tiny heroes are nature's pest control, keeping your plants safe from harm while promoting a healthy ecosystem. Take ladybugs, for example. Known for their bright red shells and black spots, ladybugs are voracious predators of aphids. A single ladybug can consume up to fifty aphids a day, making them invaluable allies in your garden. By inviting these natural predators into your space, you reduce the need for chemical interventions, allowing your plants to flourish unscathed.

Bees are another group of beneficial insects that deserve your attention. These buzzing pollinators are essential for the reproduction of many plants, including fruits and vegetables. Without bees, your garden's productivity would plummet. They transfer pollen from flower to flower, ensuring that your plants can produce the bountiful harvests you desire. To attract bees, plant a variety of flowering plants that bloom at different times throughout the season. This not only provides bees with a continuous food source but also enables your garden to remain a vibrant tapestry of color and life.

Creating an inviting environment for beneficial wildlife begins with understanding their needs. A diverse array of flowering plants will provide nectar and habitat, drawing in insects and other creatures. Consider planting native species, as they are often best suited to support local wildlife. Additionally, water sources like shallow dishes or small ponds should be provided. These water features not only quench the thirst of insects but also attract birds, which can help control pest populations. Ensuring that your garden offers the essentials—food, water, and shelter—encourages beneficial wildlife to take up residence, creating a self-sustaining ecosystem.

Maintaining a balanced ecosystem in your garden is critical for its long-term health. Encouraging natural predator-prey relationships helps keep pest populations in check without the need for chemicals. For instance, a healthy population of birds can help control caterpillars that might otherwise damage your crops. At the same time, minimizing chemical use protects beneficial species from harm. Many pesticides, even organic ones, can inadvertently kill the very insects you want to keep. By reducing your reliance on such products, you allow nature to find its own balance, leading to a healthier, more resilient garden.

You can adopt several garden practices to support beneficial insects and wildlife. Installing insect hotels provides shelter for solitary bees and other beneficial insects. These structures, often made from hollow reeds or drilled wood, offer a safe place for insects to rest and reproduce. Adding birdhouses can encourage birds to nest in your garden, offering a natural form of pest control. Additionally, allowing some areas of your garden to remain wild can create a haven for beneficial creatures. These untamed spaces offer refuge and resources that a manicured garden may lack.

As we wrap up this chapter on natural pest and disease management, consider the broader picture: your garden isn't just a collection of plants but a vibrant ecosystem. By fostering a welcoming environment for beneficial insects and wildlife, you contribute to a balanced, thriving garden. These practices enhance your garden's health and align with sustainable gardening principles. As we move forward, let's explore how to maximize your garden's productivity and beauty with creative planting and design strategies.

Chapter Nine

Seasonal Planting and Harvesting

Picture the anticipation of the first tender sprouts breaking through the soil in spring or the satisfaction of a bountiful harvest in late summer. These moments' timing hinges on understanding nature's rhythm, mainly the frost dates. These dates act as a gardener's calendar, guiding you on when to plant your seeds and when to brace your garden for the chill of frost. Grasping the concept of frost dates can transform your gardening experience, allowing you to plan effectively and maximize your garden's yield.

Knowing the last frost date in spring is crucial for starting your warm-season crops. This date marks the end of the frost threat, giving you the green light to plant tender vegetables like tomatoes and peppers that crave the sun's warmth. Conversely, the first frost date in fall signals the time to begin harvesting or protecting your plants from the impending cold. This knowledge lets you extend the growing season for cool-season crops like kale and broccoli, which can handle a touch of frost. By aligning your planting and harvesting activities with these dates, you create a roadmap that ensures your garden thrives throughout the seasons.

Calculating your local frost dates doesn't require guesswork. With the help of online tools and local agricultural extensions, you can pinpoint these dates with surprising accuracy. Websites like Dave's Garden offer a simple way to look up the first and last frost dates by entering your zip code. This information is sourced directly from the National Weather Service, providing reliable data. Additionally, consulting historical weather data can offer insights into trends and anomalies, helping you adjust your plans accordingly. By understanding these local nuances, you gain a strategic advantage, allowing you to make informed decisions about when to plant and harvest.

Frost dates also profoundly impact your planting schedules and crop selection. Cool-season crops like lettuce and spinach should be planted before the last frost date. These hardy plants can withstand a bit of chill, allowing you to start your garden early in the season. On the flip side, warm-season crops like tomatoes and cucumbers must wait until after the last frost to make sure they don't suffer from the cold. By timing your plantings around these dates, you can maximize your garden's productivity and enjoy a steady supply of fresh produce.

Microclimates add another layer of complexity to planting schedules. These are localized climate variations that can alter your gardening plans. For instance, areas near walls or buildings tend to be warmer and may protect plants from frost, allowing you to plant earlier than in more exposed locations. Pay attention to these subtle differences in your garden, as they can offer opportunities to extend your growing season or protect sensitive plants from harsh conditions. Adjusting your planting schedule to account for these microclimates can make all the difference in achieving a successful harvest.

Frost Date Lookup Exercise

Take a moment to find your local frost dates using an online tool like Dave's Garden. Note these dates in your gardening journal or calendar. Consider how these dates influence your planting plans and whether there are any microclimates in your garden that could offer additional planting opportunities. This exercise will help you align your gardening activities with nature's timing, ensuring a bountiful and well-timed harvest.

Choosing the Best Varieties for Each Season

When it comes to gardening, choosing the right plant varieties for each season is like picking the right clothes for the weather—it makes all the difference. Each season brings its own set of conditions, and selecting plants that thrive under these conditions is essential for a successful garden. Cool-season crops such as lettuce, spinach, and broccoli take center stage in early spring and fall. These plants thrive in cooler temperatures and can withstand a light frost, which makes them perfect for these transitional periods. As the days grow longer and the temperatures rise, warm-season crops like tomatoes, peppers, and squash are ready to bask in the sun's warmth. They require the heat of late spring and summer to flourish, producing vibrant fruits and vegetables that are the hallmark of summer gardens. It is imperative to align your plant choices with the season's natural rhythm so your garden remains productive and bountiful throughout the year.

Climate plays a significant role in determining which plant varieties will flourish in your garden. Selecting heat-tolerant plants is essential if you live in an area with hot, dry summers. Varieties like okra, eggplant, and certain chili peppers are well-suited to these conditions, often requiring less water and thriving under intense sunlight. In contrast, gardeners in colder regions should focus on frost-resistant cultivars that can endure chilly nights and unexpected cold snaps. Plants such as kale, Brussels sprouts, and certain types of cabbage have been bred to withstand frost, offering the resilience needed to survive harsh climates. By choosing plants that are well-adapted to your local conditions, you not only increase your chances of success but also reduce the need for interventions like excessive watering or frost protection.

The decision between heirloom and hybrid varieties is another consideration for gardeners. Heirloom plants are cherished for their rich flavors and genetic diversity. These varieties have been passed down through generations, offering unique tastes and appearances that standard hybrids might lack. However, heirlooms can be more susceptible to diseases, requiring attentive care. On the other hand, hybrid varieties are bred for specific traits, such as disease resistance and higher yields. While they may lack the distinct flavors of heirlooms, they often provide a more reliable harvest, making them a popular choice for gardeners facing challenging conditions. Balancing the benefits and drawbacks of each type allows you to tailor your garden to your personal preferences and needs.

When it comes to a specific variety of recommendations, there are some tried-and-true options that gardeners love. 'Red Russian' kale stands out for its winter hardiness, producing tender leaves that sweeten with frost. It's a versatile green that can be used in salads, soups, and stews, providing a nutritious boost to winter meals. For a burst of summer sweetness, 'Sun Gold' cherry tomatoes are a favorite. These small, golden fruits are incredibly sweet and flavorful, often enjoyed straight from the vine or added to salads for a pop of color. Their vigorous growth and abundant yields make them a staple in many summer gardens, offering a taste of sunshine in every bite. Choosing these varieties not only enhances your garden's productivity but also enriches your culinary experiences, bringing fresh, homegrown flavors to your table.

Techniques for Extending the Growing Season

Imagine having fresh, homegrown produce at your fingertips nearly all year round. By extending your growing season, you can make this dream a reality. Season extension techniques allow you to defy the calendar, stretching the productive life of your garden beyond its usual limits. One popular method is using cold frames, which are essentially unheated mini-greenhouses that protect young plants from frost and keep the soil warm. These structures can be made from old windows or clear plastic stretched over a wooden frame, creating a cozy environment for your seedlings. Cold frames capture sunlight and trap heat, providing a nurturing space for seedlings to grow strong before they're transplanted outdoors.

Another effective tool in your arsenal is row covers, which act like a warm blanket for your crops. These lightweight fabrics insulate plants during cooler months, protecting them from frost and chilly winds. They're easy to drape over rows of plants and can be secured with rocks or garden staples. The beauty of row covers lies in their simplicity and versatility—they can be removed during the day to allow air circulation and pollination, then replaced at night for warmth. By using these covers, you can give your plants a head start in spring and extend their growing period into the fall, making the most of every precious day.

For those ready to take it up a notch, constructing protective structures like hoop houses can be a game-changer. Made from PVC pipes and plastic sheeting, these DIY projects are like mini greenhouses that trap heat and protect plants from extreme weather. They're excellent for growing heat-loving crops during cooler months. Building a hoop house involves bending flexible PVC pipes into arches and covering them with clear plastic. This creates a tunnel-like structure that shields plants from the elements while letting in sunlight. Another option is using cloches—small, portable covers that protect individual plants. These can be as simple as a cut-off plastic bottle placed over a plant, providing a microclimate that keeps frost at bay.

Beyond structural solutions, succession planting is another strategy to maximize your garden's output. By staggering your plantings, you can enjoy a continuous harvest throughout the season. For example, sow a new batch of lettuce every two weeks to guarantee a steady supply of fresh greens. This method is particularly effective for fast-growing crops like radishes and spinach, which can be harvested and replaced quickly. Planning your plantings in waves keeps your garden productive and your table full of fresh produce. It's all about timing your plantings to take advantage of the varying conditions throughout the season so there's always something ready to harvest.

Of course, extending the growing season comes with its own set of challenges. Managing humidity and ventilation in covered structures is vital to prevent mold and mildew. It's important to monitor the conditions inside these structures and adjust as needed. For instance, open the ends of your hoop houses on warm days to allow fresh air to circulate. Similarly, be wary of overheating your plants in late spring. Shade cloths can help mitigate this by filtering sunlight and reducing temperature, ensuring your plants remain comfortable. Balancing these factors ensures your garden remains healthy and productive, allowing you to enjoy the fruits of your labor long after the traditional growing season has ended.

Harvesting Tips for Maximum Yield and Freshness

Harvesting is like the grand finale of your gardening efforts, a moment where all the care and nurturing you've given your plants culminate in a rewarding yield. Timing and technique are everything to get the best out of your garden. Take leafy greens, for instance. Harvest them in the morning, when they're at their freshest, crisp from the night's cooler temperatures. Morning harvesting helps preserve the greens' texture and flavor, ensuring they're at their peak when they hit your plate. Similarly, tomatoes should be picked when they're fully ripe, bursting with flavor, and ready to delight your taste buds. This careful timing not only improves the taste but also maximizes the nutritional benefits of your produce.

Post-harvest handling is another crucial step in maintaining the quality of your garden's bounty. Root vegetables, like carrots and beets, benefit from breathable bags that allow air circulation, preventing mold and prolonging freshness. Herbs, on the other hand, need a different approach. To keep them fresh, place them in a jar of water, much like a bouquet of flowers, and pop them in the fridge. This simple trick extends their life and keeps them vibrant until you're ready to use them in your cooking. Proper storage techniques make certain that the fruits of your labor remain delicious and nutritious long after they leave the garden.

When it comes to surplus produce, preserving what you can't consume right away is key. Freezing is a fantastic option for many vegetables. Start by blanching them—briefly boiling them to stop enzyme action, then cooling them in ice water. This process locks in flavor, color, and nutrients, making your veggies freezer-ready for those months when your garden isn't producing. Herbs and fruits can be dehydrated for long-term storage. You can concentrate their flavors using a dehydrator, creating dried herbs for seasoning or fruit snacks that pack a punch. These preservation methods reduce waste and allow you to savor the taste of summer, even in the depths of winter.

Avoiding common harvesting mistakes is essential for a successful yield. One such error is using the wrong tools, leading to damaged plants and reduced harvests. Invest in good-quality garden scissors or pruners to make clean cuts, minimizing plant harm and encouraging continued growth. Another pitfall is not recognizing signs of overripeness, which can lead to spoilage and attract pests. Pay close attention to your crops, harvesting them at their prime to guarantee they're at their best. By learning to read the signs, you can prevent these issues and make the most of your garden's offerings.

Harvesting Checklist

Create a checklist to guide your harvesting process. Include tasks like checking the ripeness of each crop, using the right tools, and following proper storage techniques. This list helps streamline the process, ensuring nothing is overlooked, and your produce remains top-notch.

As you stand in your garden, basket in hand, remember that each step in the harvesting process is a chance to connect with your plants. Your careful planning and attentiveness yield delicious produce and create a deeper appreciation for the cycle of growth and renewal. With these tips in mind, you're well-equipped to enjoy the fruits of your labor, savoring each bite of homegrown goodness.

Chapter Ten

Building Community and Sharing Knowledge

Have you ever noticed how gardens have a way of bringing people together? There's something magical about how a shared love for plants can foster friendships, build communities, and even transform neighborhoods. Community gardens, especially those with raised beds, offer an excellent opportunity to experience this magic firsthand. They're not just about growing vegetables; they're about growing connections. These gardens serve as vibrant green spaces that provide everyone—from enthusiastic beginners to seasoned gardeners—a chance to learn, share, and thrive together.

Community gardens are more than plots of land for planting; they are social hubs where collaboration and camaraderie flourish. When you participate in a community garden, you become part of a supportive network that encourages knowledge exchange and collective problem-solving. Whether swapping tips on pest control or sharing excess zucchini, the social connections formed here are invaluable. These gardens also offer access to fresh produce, which is particularly beneficial in urban areas where grocery stores might be sparse. By growing your food, you gain a sense of empowerment and self-sufficiency while reducing your carbon footprint—a win-win for you and the planet!

Planning and organizing a community garden requires thoughtful consideration and a bit of groundwork. The first step is securing a suitable location. Look for a spot that receives ample sunlight and has access to water. Once you've identified the perfect place, you'll need to navigate the process of obtaining permits and permissions from local authorities. This may involve liaising with city officials or neighborhood associations to ensure compliance with zoning regulations. Establishing a governance structure with clear rules is essential for maintaining harmony within the garden—set guidelines for plot usage, maintenance schedules, and conflict resolution. Engaging with potential members and stakeholders early on is also key. Host informational meetings to gauge interest and gather input on the garden's design and function.

Designing the layout of the community garden is where you can get creative. Consider the needs of all gardeners, ensuring the space is accessible and inclusive. Shared pathways that weave through the raised beds facilitate movement and invite exploration and interaction. These paths should be wide enough for wheelchairs and strollers, making the garden accessible to people of all ages and abilities. Allocating individual plots alongside communal planting areas balances personal space and collective efforts. While individual plots allow gardeners to focus on their projects, communal areas encourage collaboration and shared experiences. These communal spaces can house larger crops or ornamental plants that everyone can enjoy.

Challenges are inevitable in any community project, but they can be managed effectively with the right approach. Conflict may arise over plot allocation or maintenance responsibilities, so having a clear governance structure helps address these issues. Achieve equitable access by rotating plot assignments or implementing a lottery system. Maintenance can also be a point of contention, but organizing regular work days fosters a sense of shared responsibility. Encourage open communication to resolve disagreements and promote a positive atmosphere. Community gardens thrive when everyone feels valued and heard, so nurturing an inclusive and respectful environment is paramount.

Community Garden Planning Checklist

- Location and Permits: Identify a sunny, accessible location and secure necessary permits.

- Governance Structure: Establish clear rules and roles for plot usage and maintenance.

- Engagement: Host meetings to engage potential members and gather input.

- Design and Layout: Create accessible pathways and allocate individual and communal plots.

- Conflict and Maintenance: Implement strategies for equitable access and shared responsibilities.

By working together, community gardens become vibrant ecosystems of learning, sharing, and connection. They are places where you can cultivate not just plants but friendships and community spirit.

Hosting Workshops and Garden Tours

Imagine walking through a vibrant garden, learning about plants and techniques from fellow enthusiasts. This is the magic of hosting workshops and garden tours. They aren't just about imparting knowledge; they're about creating a community united by a shared passion for gardening. Workshops provide an ideal platform for sharing best practices and innovative techniques, enhancing everyone's gardening skills. They offer a space where seasoned gardeners can pass down their wisdom while newcomers can ask questions and gain confidence. This exchange of ideas fosters a sense of camaraderie, building a community with a shared purpose. A well-organized workshop can also attract new members, inviting them to join the gardening initiative and contribute to its growth.

Planning a workshop requires a little forethought and a lot of enthusiasm. Start by identifying topics that resonate with your community's needs and interests. Perhaps there's a desire to learn about natural pest control or the intricacies of composting. Once you've settled on a theme, seek knowledgeable speakers or facilitators who can engage and inspire. These could be local experts or experienced gardeners willing to share their insights. Promoting the event is key to its success. Leverage local networks, community bulletin boards, and social media to spread the word. Create eye-catching flyers or digital invites to pique interest and reach a broader audience.

Garden tours, on the other hand, offer a more interactive and visually engaging experience. They allow participants to see gardening techniques in action and ask questions on the spot. Preparing your garden for a tour involves a bit of sprucing up. Make sure paths are clear, plants are well-tended, and educational displays are ready to go. Consider creating informational materials or guides that participants can take home. These might include plant lists, care tips, or even a map of the garden layout. Scheduling tours to accommodate different group sizes and interests is something to consider. You can offer multiple time slots or themed tours, like a morning walk focusing on pollinators or an evening stroll highlighting aromatic herbs.

Hosting these events isn't without its challenges. Ensuring accessibility and safety for all participants is paramount. Make sure paths are clear and easy to navigate, with no tripping hazards. For those with mobility issues, provide seating areas or alternative viewing spots. Managing group sizes is another consideration. Too many participants can lead to congestion and hamper the experience. Consider capping attendance and offering multiple sessions if interest is high. This way, everyone can engage fully without feeling rushed or crowded.

Workshop and Tour Planning Tips

- Relevance: Tailor content to community interests and needs.

- Engagement: Use local networks and social media for promotion.

- Accessibility: Ensure paths are clear and provide seating for those in need.

- Flexibility: Offer multiple time slots to manage group sizes and interests.

Bringing people together through workshops and tours not only enriches their knowledge but also strengthens community bonds. As participants leave inspired and informed, they carry with them a renewed enthusiasm for gardening and a deeper connection to their community.

Engaging with Online Gardening Communities

In today's digital age, the gardening community isn't confined to your local neighborhood; it spans the globe. Online platforms have opened doors to a wealth of knowledge and networking opportunities that were once unimaginable. Engaging with these online gardening communities can be a game-changer for anyone looking to enhance their gardening skills and connect with fellow enthusiasts. The beauty of these spaces lies in their diversity. You can access advice from experts and novice gardeners alike, each offering unique insights and experiences. Whether you're troubleshooting a stubborn pest problem or seeking inspiration for your next project, these digital forums are treasure troves of information. Participating in global discussions allows you to learn about gardening practices from different climates and cultures, broadening your perspective and perhaps sparking new ideas for your own garden. Sharing your successes and challenges with a broad audience provides personal satisfaction and contributes to the community's collective learning.

Finding your niche in the vast landscape of online gardening communities can be an exciting adventure. Platforms like Facebook and Reddit host a myriad of groups dedicated to various aspects of gardening. Whether your interest lies in organic gardening, permaculture, or even the cultivation of rare orchids, a group likely caters to your passion. Begin by searching for keywords related to your interests and join groups that resonate with you. Specialized forums can also be valuable resources; they often foster more focused discussions and a sense of camaraderie among members. The key is to engage with communities that align with your interests and values, creating a supportive network that enriches your gardening journey.

Active participation in these online spaces is where the real magic happens. Sharing your experiences and photos of personal gardening projects can inspire others while also inviting feedback and suggestions. It's an excellent way to celebrate successes and learn from setbacks. Asking and answering questions is another powerful way to engage. By supporting fellow members, you contribute to a culture of knowledge-sharing and collaboration. Many communities also host virtual events, webinars, or gardening challenges that offer opportunities to deepen your knowledge and connect with others. These events can introduce you to new techniques and perspectives, further enhancing your gardening expertise.

Navigating the online world isn't without its challenges. Misinformation and conflicting advice can sometimes muddy the waters. It's important to approach online information critically, verifying claims with trusted sources and considering the context of your own garden. Engaging in respectful and constructive dialogue is imperative. Disagreements may arise, but maintaining a positive and open-minded attitude fosters a healthy community environment. Remember, everyone is at a different stage in their gardening journey, and patience and kindness go a long way in building meaningful connections. As you contribute and participate, you'll find that the support and camaraderie of online gardening communities can be as rewarding as the gardens themselves.

Sharing Seeds and Resources Locally

Seed sharing is like exchanging tiny packets of potential. Each seed carries a story waiting to unfold, a connection to past gardeners who have nurtured and passed it down through generations. By exchanging seeds, you help preserve heirloom and rare plant varieties, ensuring their continued existence and diversity in our gardens. These heirlooms often bring unique flavors and resilience, enriching our gardens with history and variety. Moreover, swapping seeds and resources with fellow gardeners can significantly reduce gardening costs. Instead of purchasing new packets every season, you can trade seeds with others, saving money while expanding your collection. This practice not only lightens the financial load but also encourages experimentation. Trying out new plant varieties you might not have considered before can lead to delightful surprises and broaden your gardening horizons.

Organizing seed swaps and resource exchanges requires some planning, but it's a rewarding endeavor that strengthens community ties. Start by securing a venue that's convenient and accessible. This could be a community center, library, or even someone's spacious backyard. Once you have a location, set a date that accommodates as many participants as possible. Establish clear guidelines for the event, such as the types of seeds accepted, the number of seeds to bring, and the process for exchanging them. Transparency in guidelines ensures everyone knows what to expect and fosters a fair exchange. Promoting the swap is essential to attract participants.

Utilize local networks, flyers, social media, and gardening groups to spread the word and generate excitement.

Resource pooling goes beyond seeds; it extends to tools and materials that can enhance community gardening efforts. Creating communal tool libraries or lending systems allows gardeners to access equipment they might not own, like tillers or special pruners. This approach reduces individual costs and encourages resource sharing, fostering a sense of community ownership. Similarly, organizing bulk purchases of soil amendments or seeds can save money and will help everyone achieve access to quality materials. By pooling resources, you not only support each other but also strengthen the community garden as a whole, making it a more sustainable and interconnected space.

However, sharing resources comes with its own set of challenges. Ensuring fair exchanges is critical to maintaining trust and engagement. Implementing a system where participants can track borrowed tools or contribute equally to seed swaps can prevent misunderstandings. Managing the quality and viability of shared seeds is another consideration. Encourage participants to label seeds accurately and provide information about their growth history. This transparency helps maintain the integrity of the exchange and guarantees everyone benefits from healthy, viable seeds.

As we wrap up this chapter on building community and sharing knowledge, remember that gardening is as much about connecting with others as it is about growing plants. Sharing seeds and resources not only enriches our gardens but also strengthens the bonds within our community. In the next chapter, we'll explore the practical aspects of maintaining a thriving raised bed garden, focusing on soil health, pest management, and more.

Chapter Eleven

Troubleshooting and Problem Solving

Imagine strolling through your garden only to discover that your once-vibrant plants are looking a bit under the weather. Perhaps their leaves are wilting, or you notice unusual spots appearing. It's frustrating, right? Understanding plant health issues is essential for any gardener, and recognizing the signs early can make all the difference. Let's dive into common symptoms of distress and how to figure out what's going wrong.

Wilting leaves might seem straightforward—they need water, right? But what if you've been diligent with your watering routine, and they still look sad? Wilting can signal deeper issues, such as root damage or even overwatering, which can suffocate roots by depriving them of oxygen. Pay attention to the soil: if it's consistently soggy, you might be drowning your plants instead of hydrating them. On the other hand, dry, crumbly soil might indicate the need for watering. Always check rot and reduced oxygen availability. Understanding the root of these problems is your first step to a healthier garden.

Several factors contribute to poor drainage. Compacted soil is a major culprit, as it prevents water from seeping through, creating a soggy mess that can suffocate plant roots. Soil composition is another factor; a mix that's too heavy in clay can hold water, while overly sandy soil lets it flow away too quickly. Even the construction of your raised bed can affect drainage. If the bed isn't elevated enough or lacks proper outlets for excess water, you may encounter problems. Addressing these causes requires a multi-faceted approach, focusing on improving both soil structure and bed design.

Enhancing drainage in your raised beds doesn't have to be a daunting task. Start by incorporating coarse sand or organic matter like compost into your soil. This improves the soil's structure, allowing water to move more freely and providing better root aeration. If your beds are consistently waterlogged, consider elevating them further. Adding height can prevent water accumulation, especially in areas prone to heavy rain. Perforated pipes, strategically placed at the base of your beds, can also aid in water movement. These pipes act like channels, guiding excess water away from your plant roots and ensuring a healthier growing environment.

Preventive measures are key to avoiding drainage issues from the start. When constructing your raised beds, ensure they're properly graded with a slight slope to facilitate water runoff. This simple step helps direct water flow away from the beds, minimizing pooling risk. Regularly aerating the soil is another essential practice. By loosening the soil, you maintain its porosity, allowing air and water to circulate freely. This improves drainage and enhances root health, leading to more vigorous plant growth.

Building your beds with drainage in mind ensures they remain a thriving home for your plants. Assessing and addressing drainage problems can save you from future headaches and keep your garden flourishing. Remember, a little effort upfront can prevent big issues down the line, allowing you to enjoy the fruits of your labor without the worry of waterlogged soil.

Combating Nutrient Deficiencies and Imbalances

Nutrient deficiencies can be a real thorn in the side of any gardener. They sneak up on your plants, often showing subtle signs that can be mistaken for other issues. The impact, however, can be severe. Imagine a garden full of stunted plants struggling to flower or bear fruit. This scenario is often the result of a phosphorus deficiency. Phosphorus plays an important role in energy transfer within plants; without it, growth stagnates, and flowering is minimal. Conversely, iron shortages lead to chlorosis, where leaves turn yellow while veins remain green. This condition hampers photosynthesis, weakening plants over time. Both scenarios highlight how nutrient imbalances can drastically affect productivity.

Identifying these deficiencies isn't as daunting as it may seem. Conducting regular soil tests is one of the most effective ways to pinpoint what your soil might be lacking. These tests provide a snapshot of nutrient levels, guiding you on what amendments are necessary. If you notice specific symptoms, like yellowing leaves, consulting a detailed guide on plant nutrient needs can help. Observing your plants closely and understanding their symptoms is a skill worth cultivating. This way, you can act swiftly to address imbalances before they cause significant harm.

Correcting these deficiencies involves targeted amendments that replenish missing nutrients. If you're dealing with chlorosis, applying chelated iron can make a world of difference. This form of iron is easily absorbed by plants, helping them regain their lush green color. For phosphorus deficiencies, bone meal is a fantastic choice. It not only provides phosphorus but also adds calcium, another vital nutrient for healthy plant development. Incorporating these amendments into your soil will help your plants receive the nutrients they need to thrive. It's like giving them a much-needed boost, restoring vitality, and promoting robust growth.

Maintaining balanced soil nutrition requires a proactive approach. Regular soil testing is key, as it allows you to monitor nutrient levels and adjust your amendments accordingly. An amendment schedule can be particularly helpful, ensuring that your soil remains fertile throughout the growing season. Crop rotation also plays a crucial role in nutrient management. By changing the types of plants grown in each area, you naturally balance nutrient demands, preventing depletion. For instance, following nitrogen-heavy feeders like corn with legumes helps replenish soil nitrogen levels. This practice keeps your soil healthy and supports sustainable gardening.

Creating a nutrient-rich environment is like setting the stage for a successful performance. Each plant gets what it needs to flourish, resulting in a garden that's not only productive but also resilient. As you tend to your garden, remember that nutrient management is an ongoing process. By staying vigilant and responsive to your plants' needs, you cultivate a thriving space where every leaf and blossom tells a story of care and nourishment.

Managing Unexpected Weather Conditions

Gardening often dances to the whims of the weather, and as much as we'd like to control it, Mother Nature has her own plans. Sudden weather changes can throw even the most seasoned gardener a curveball. One day, your plants are basking in the gentle warmth of spring; the next, they're shivering in an unexpected frost. Early spring plantings are particularly vulnerable to frost damage, with tender shoots turning black and wilting overnight if caught unprotected. On the flip side, an unexpected heatwave in the heart of summer can lead to heat stress, causing leaves to curl and plants to droop as they struggle to cope with the intense heat. These rapid changes can stress your plants, impacting their growth and productivity. By understanding these challenges, you're better equipped to help your garden weather the storm—literally.

When faced with these unpredictable weather swings, having a toolkit of strategies can make all the difference. For those cold snaps that threaten to undo your hard work, row covers, or frost blankets are your garden's best friends. These can be quickly draped over plants, providing a protective barrier against the chill. They work by trapping heat from the ground, creating a microclimate that keeps plants safe from frost damage. Lightweight and easy to deploy, these covers can be lifesavers for early spring seedlings. On particularly hot days, shade cloths come into play. By filtering the sun's rays, they reduce heat exposure and prevent leaf scorch. Installing these cloths over your beds can help keep the soil cooler and reduce evaporation, ensuring your plants receive the hydration they need without the added stress of intense sun.

Keeping a keen eye on weather patterns is another proactive step you can take. Local weather forecasts and alerts are invaluable resources, helping you anticipate and prepare for sudden changes. Make it a habit to check these forecasts regularly, especially during transitional seasons when the weather is most unpredictable. If a frost is predicted, you can adjust your planting schedules accordingly, delaying planting sensitive crops until the risk of frost has passed. Similarly, knowing when a heatwave is on the horizon allows you to water deeply and mulch well in advance, giving your plants a better chance to withstand the heat. By staying informed, you turn potential surprises into manageable events, reducing the impact on your garden.

Long-term, adapting to climate variability is about building resilience in your garden. Selecting climate-tolerant plant varieties is a savvy move. These plants are bred to withstand extremes, offering a buffer against unexpected weather. For example, drought-tolerant varieties can thrive with less water, making them ideal for regions prone to dry spells. Designing your garden with windbreaks can also protect against harsh winds that can dry out plants and erode soil. Hedges, fences, or even strategically placed rows of taller plants can act as shields, reducing wind impact and creating a more stable environment for your garden. Water management systems, like rain barrels, can capture and store rainwater, providing a valuable resource during dry periods.

Creating a garden that can withstand the uncertainty of weather requires planning and foresight. By employing these strategies, you not only protect your current crops but also set the stage for a robust, adaptable garden that can flourish in varied conditions. The goal is to work with nature, rather than against it, finding harmony between your gardening aspirations and the natural world's rhythms.

Chapter Twelve

Sustainable Practices for Long-Term Success

I magine turning your kitchen scraps and garden waste into a rich, earthy compost that nourishes your plants and reduces your carbon footprint. Composting is like nature's way of recycling, transforming organic materials into a valuable resource for your garden. Composting contributes to a healthier planet by keeping waste out of landfills and enriching your soil with essential nutrients. Think of it as giving back to the earth, closing the sustainability loop, and creating a thriving environment for your garden.

Starting a compost system might seem daunting, but it can be surprisingly simple and adaptable to your space. Whether you have a sprawling backyard or a compact urban garden, there's a composting method that suits your needs. Open piles are great if you have room to spare, allowing for easy turning and aeration. Consider a compost bin or tumbler for smaller spaces, which keeps things tidy and contained. When selecting materials, aim for a balance of "browns" and "greens." Browns include dead leaves, straw, and shredded paper, which are rich in carbon and vital for compost structure. Greens, like vegetable peels, coffee grounds, and grass clippings, provide the nitrogen that fuels decomposition. Together, they create the perfect recipe for compost success.

Speeding up the composting process involves a bit of science and a touch of art. Shredding materials increases surface area, allowing microbes to break them down more efficiently. Picture your compost pile as a living organism that breathes and eats. It needs the right balance of air and moisture to thrive. Keep your pile as moist as a wrung-out sponge and turn it regularly to ensure aeration. This process introduces oxygen, which is essential for the microbes that decompose organic matter. By maintaining these conditions, you'll soon have a dark, crumbly compost ready to enrich your soil.

Composting isn't without its challenges, but you can overcome common issues with a few tweaks. One frequent problem is odor, often caused by an imbalance of carbon and nitrogen. If your compost smells like ammonia, it's time to add more browns. On the flip side, if decomposition slows and the pile seems dry, add more greens and a splash of water. Pests can also be a concern, especially when composting food scraps. Secure lids and barriers can keep unwanted critters at bay while turning the pile regularly discourages them from settling in.

Trench composting is another technique to consider, especially if you want to enrich your raised beds directly. This method involves digging a trench in your garden bed and layering organic materials like leaves and kitchen scraps. Cover the trench with soil and let nature do the rest. Over time, the materials break down, releasing nutrients directly into the soil. This method is particularly useful at the end of the growing season, allowing the compost to mature before the next planting cycle. It's a cost-effective way to maintain soil levels and reduce the need for store-bought compost, making the most of your garden waste. However, avoid materials like meat or rice, which can attract pests or harbor bacteria.

By embracing composting, you're not just feeding your plants; you're fostering a sustainable cycle that benefits the environment and your garden. This practice aligns with the ethos of raised bed gardening, emphasizing efficiency and resourcefulness. As you turn waste into nourishment, you contribute to a greener future, one compost pile at a time.

Composting Checklist

- Materials: Gather a mix of browns (leaves, straw) and greens (vegetable scraps, coffee grounds).

- Composting System: Choose between an open pile, bin, or tumbler based on your space.

- Moisture and Aeration: Maintain moisture like a wrung-out sponge; turn regularly for aeration.

- Odor Management: Balance carbon and nitrogen; add more browns if it smells like ammonia.

- Pest Prevention: Use secure lids and barriers; avoid composting meat or greasy food scraps.

With these steps, you're well on your way to creating a sustainable, thriving garden.

Using Mulch to Conserve Water and Suppress Weeds

Mulching is like giving your garden a cozy blanket, offering protection and nutrients while keeping weeds at bay. One of the most immediate benefits of using mulch is its ability to conserve moisture. By covering the soil, mulch reduces evaporation, ensuring that your plants have a steady supply of water even during the hotter months. This moisture retention is invaluable, especially in regions prone to drought or for gardeners who may not have the time to water frequently. Mulch also serves as a natural weed suppressant by blocking sunlight, which prevents weed seeds from germinating. This reduces competition for nutrients and space, allowing your garden plants to thrive without the constant battle against unwanted greenery.

Selecting the right mulch is necessary for its effectiveness. Organic mulches, such as straw, wood chips, and shredded leaves, are popular choices for their dual benefits of moisture retention and nutrient contribution as they break down. Straw is especially favored for its ability to regulate soil temperature and its relatively quick decomposition, enriching the soil within a year. Wood chips provide a long-lasting cover that slowly releases nutrients as they decompose. Shredded leaves enrich the soil and create a barrier against weeds. For those who prefer something more permanent, inorganic mulches like gravel or landscape fabric can effectively maintain soil structure and provide a clean, finished look to your garden. However, they don't contribute nutrients as organic options do.

Applying mulch correctly is key to reaping its full benefits. Spread the mulch evenly across your raised beds, aiming for a consistent layer of about 2 to 4 inches thick. This depth helps suppress weeds while retaining moisture without suffocating the soil. Be mindful to keep mulch a few inches away from plant stems and trunks to prevent rot. Excessive moisture around the base of plants can lead to fungal diseases or decay, so a little breathing room is imperative. For best results, apply mulch in the spring after the soil has warmed or in the fall to protect the soil over winter. Regularly check your mulch layer and replenish it as needed, especially after heavy rains or strong winds that may displace it.

While mulching offers many benefits, it does come with potential drawbacks that require attention. Organic mulches decompose over time and will need replenishment, which is a natural process that enriches the soil. However, as they break down, they may also attract pests like slugs and snails, which thrive in the cool, moist environment mulch creates. To manage this, you can lay down slug traps or encourage natural predators like birds to visit your garden. Monitoring the mulch for signs of pest activity and adjusting your garden's balance can help maintain a healthy ecosystem. Additionally, if your mulch layer becomes too thick, it might retain excess moisture, potentially leading to root rot. Simply fluff the mulch regularly to assist with proper airflow and drainage.

Mulching is not just a gardening task; it's an ongoing relationship with your garden that requires observation and adjustment. The benefits of using mulch are substantial, from conserving water and reducing weeds to improving soil fertility. It's a simple yet powerful way to enhance your garden's health and sustainability, making it a must-do for any gardener looking to cultivate a thriving raised bed garden.

Incorporating Permaculture Principles into Your Garden

Have you ever looked at a thriving forest and wondered how it flourishes year after year without human intervention? That's essentially the magic of permaculture, a concept that encourages creating self-sustaining ecosystems by mimicking nature's own systems. At its core, permaculture is about designing gardens that require minimal external inputs by maximizing resource efficiency. Imagine a garden where plants, animals, and insects coexist harmoniously, each playing a role that supports the entire ecosystem. This isn't just an ideal; it's achievable through thoughtful garden design that emphasizes ecological balance.

Designing a permaculture-based garden in raised beds starts with zoning plants based on their needs and functions. Think of your garden as a series of zones, each with its own set of priorities and functions. Place high-maintenance plants, like vegetables that require frequent care, in zones that are easily accessible. Reserve less accessible areas for low-maintenance plants, such as perennials or native species, that thrive with little intervention. This strategic placement reduces the time and energy you spend tending to your garden while ensuring all plants receive the care they need. Companion planting and polyculture techniques further enhance biodiversity. By growing a variety of plants together, you can create a resilient garden that naturally resists pests and diseases. For example, pairing marigolds with tomatoes deters harmful insects and brings vibrant color to your garden. This approach encourages a diverse range of organisms, from pollinators to beneficial insects, to call your garden home.

Water management is another critical component of permaculture. Clever techniques like swales and contour planting achieve efficient water use and conservation. Swales are shallow trenches designed to capture and redirect rainwater, allowing it to seep slowly into the soil. By placing swales on contour lines, you can control water flow and prevent erosion, creating a more stable environment for your plants. Greywater systems offer another sustainable option, recycling water from baths, sinks, and washing machines for irrigation. By integrating these systems, you conserve valuable resources and reduce your environmental footprint, ensuring that your garden thrives even in dry conditions.

Permaculture also embraces the idea of integrating wildlife habitats into your garden. Attracting beneficial wildlife supports garden health by creating a balanced ecosystem. Picture a garden buzzing with bees and butterflies; their presence is a testament to the thriving pollinator habitats you've created. By planting native species, you provide food and shelter for local fauna, encouraging them to take up residence in your garden. These animals help control pest populations, reducing the need for chemical interventions. Birdhouses, bee hotels, and water features further enhance your garden's appeal to wildlife, transforming it into a sanctuary for all creatures, great and small. This partnership between plants and wildlife fosters a dynamic, self-regulating environment that aligns with permaculture's principles.

By incorporating permaculture techniques into your raised bed garden, you create an ecosystem that's productive and sustainable. This approach encourages you to work with nature rather than against it, leading to a garden that thrives with minimal effort. Whether you're zoning plants, conserving water, or welcoming wildlife, each step brings you closer to a harmonious, self-sustaining garden. This is the essence of permaculture: a garden that nurtures itself and its surroundings, offering a model of sustainability and resilience that benefits both you and the planet.

Planning for Future Growth and Sustainability

In the ever-changing landscape of gardening, planning for future growth isn't just a smart move—it's necessary for long-term success. As gardeners, we must be forward-thinking, anticipating changes in climate and the availability of resources. Imagine your garden as a living organism that adapts and evolves, meeting the challenges of each season with resilience and strength. Setting long-term goals for productivity and sustainability helps you create a garden that thrives now and in the future. This involves everything from considering weather patterns and soil conditions to the types of plants you'll grow. By understanding and adapting to these factors, you can ensure that your garden remains a productive and vibrant space for years to come.

Creating a sustainable garden plan involves thoughtful preparation and flexibility. Start with regular soil testing to assess fertility and nutrient levels. This guarantees that your plants receive the nutrients they need throughout the growing season. Based on these results, amend your soil with the appropriate fertilizers or organic matter to maintain its health. Incorporate structures and plantings that can adapt to changing conditions. For example, using trellises for climbing plants maximizes vertical space and provides shade for heat-sensitive crops. Raised beds themselves offer flexibility, allowing you to control soil quality and drainage. Consider rotating your beds to different locations to prevent soil fatigue and improve nutrient distribution.

Succession planting is a valuable technique to keep your garden productive over time. By planning successive plantings, you can optimize your yield and enjoy a continuous harvest. This involves rotating crops to maintain soil health and prevent the buildup of pests and diseases. By staggering plantings, you make sure that as one crop is harvested, another is ready to take its place. For instance, as you pull up spring radishes, you might plant summer beans in the same spot. This maximizes productivity and keeps your garden looking full and vibrant throughout the season. Succession planting requires a keen understanding of plant growth cycles and climate conditions, but the rewards are worth the effort.

Community and collaboration play a pivotal role in sustainable gardening. Engaging with local gardening networks and initiatives allows you to share resources, knowledge, and experiences with fellow gardeners. This collaboration fosters a sense of community and encourages the exchange of seeds, tools, and expertise. By pooling resources, you can reduce costs and increase access to a wider variety of plants and materials. Participating in community gardens or gardening clubs also provides opportunities to learn from others and gain new insights into sustainable practices. This collective effort strengthens individual gardens and contributes to the overall health and resilience of local ecosystems.

Future planning in gardening is about foresight and adaptability. You establish a sustainable, thriving garden by setting long-term goals, creating dynamic plans, and engaging with your community. These practices connect your garden to a larger network of shared knowledge and resources, paving the way for a resilient future.

Conclusion

As we end our journey through the world of raised bed gardening, I hope you're feeling inspired and empowered to embark on your own gardening adventure. Throughout this book, we've explored the myriad benefits of raised bed gardening, from improved soil management and space efficiency to the ease of maintenance that comes with this sustainable approach. By now, you've got a solid understanding of how raised beds can transform your gardening experience, making it more productive, rewarding, and enjoyable.

We've covered a lot of ground together, haven't we? From the nitty-gritty of constructing your own raised beds to the art of crafting the perfect soil composition, you've gained the knowledge and skills to build a thriving garden from the ground up. You've discovered the magic of companion planting, learning how to pair plants that support each other's growth and health. And you've got a toolbox full of natural pest management techniques, ensuring that your garden stays vibrant and healthy without resorting to harsh chemicals.

But it's not just about practical skills. Throughout this book, we've emphasized the importance of sustainability in gardening practices. By embracing techniques like composting, mulching, and permaculture principles, you're not just growing a garden but cultivating a more ecological, balanced way of life. These practices aren't just good for your plants; they're good for the planet, too.

My goal with this book has been to empower you and give you the confidence and know-how to create a thriving raised bed garden, no matter your experience level or the size of your space. I've focused on practical, easy-to-follow techniques tailored to maximize space and optimize plant health. Whether you're a seasoned green thumb or a budding beginner, I hope you've found the guidance and inspiration you need to take your gardening to the next level.

But remember, gardening isn't a solo endeavor. One of the most rewarding aspects of this hobby is the sense of community it fosters. By building connections with fellow gardeners, both locally and online, you open yourself up to a world of shared knowledge, resources, and camaraderie. Don't be afraid to reach out and share your experiences, successes, and challenges. You never know what you might learn or who you might inspire.

So, what's next? It's time to take all that you've learned and put it into practice. Start small if you need to, but start. Build that first raised bed, get your hands dirty, and watch the magic unfold. Experiment with new techniques, try out different plant combinations and don't be afraid to make mistakes. That's how we learn and grow, both as gardeners and as individuals.

As you embark on this journey, know that I'm here to support you. I'd love to hear about your experiences, to see photos of your thriving gardens, and to answer any questions you might have. Connect with me and the gardening community through social media or gardening forums. Let's keep the conversation going and continue to learn from each other.

Before I sign off, I am grateful for your interest and commitment to sustainable gardening. By choosing to garden in raised beds, you're not just enhancing your own life; you're contributing to a greener, more resilient world. You're creating a space that nourishes both body and soul, and that's a wonderful thing.

So here's to you, my fellow gardener. May your beds be bountiful, your plants be healthy, and your spirit be nourished by the simple joys of watching life grow. Remember, every seed you sow and every plant you tend is a step towards a more sustainable, connected future.

Keeping the Garden Growing

Now that you have everything you need to create a thriving raised bed garden, it's time to pass on your newfound knowledge and help others discover the same success!

Simply by sharing your honest opinion of this book on Amazon, you'll guide other gardeners—whether they're beginners or seasoned growers—toward the information they need to start their own raised bed journey.

Thank you for your support! Gardening knowledge grows when we share it, and you're helping me keep that tradition alive.

To share your thoughts, please consider leaving this book a review on Amazon!

Happy Gardening!

MJ Woods

Companion Planting Guide

BASIL – Cilantro, Oregano, Peppers, Tomatoes, Sage, Thyme

BEANS – Broccoli, Carrots, Cauliflower, Celery, Cilantro, Corn, Cucumber, Peas, Potatoes, Radish, Rosemary, Sage, Squash, Strawberries, Swiss Chard, Tomatoes, Thyme

BEETS – Broccoli, Bush Beans, Cabbage, Carrots, Cauliflower, Garlic, Kale, Lettuce, Onion, Radish, Tomatoes

BROCCOLI – Beans, Beets, Carrots, Cauliflower, Chives, Cilantro, Cucumber, Dill, Garlic, Lettuce, Nasturtium, Onion, Oregano, Rosemary, Sage, Spinach, Swiss Chard, Thyme

CABBAGE – Beets, Celery, Cilantro, Garlic, Onion, Potatoes, Rosemary, Sage, Swiss Chard Thyme

CARROTS – Beans, Beets, Broccoli, Cauliflower, Chives, Garlic, Leeks, Lettuce, Onion, Parsley, Peas, Peppers, Radish, Rosemary, Sage, Thyme

CAULIFLOWER – Beans, Beets, Broccoli, Carrots, Chives, Cilantro, Cucumber, Dill, Garlic, Lettuce, Nasturtium, Onion, Oregano, Rosemary, Sage, Spinach, Swiss Chard, Thyme

CELERY – Beans, Cabbage, Chives, Cucumber, Leeks, Parsley, Spinach, Swiss Chard, Thyme, Tomatoes

CHIVES – Broccoli, Carrots, Cauliflower, Celery, Parsley, Sage, Thyme, Tomatoes

CILANTRO – Basil, Beans, Broccoli, Cabbage, Cauliflower, Dill, Kale, Lettuce, Parsley, Peas, Potatoes, Sage, Spinach, Swiss Chard, Thyme, Tomatoes

CORN – Beans, Cucumber, Dill, Melon, Parsley, Peas, Potatoes, Sage, Squash, Sunflower, Thyme

CUCUMBER – Beans, Broccoli, Cauliflower, Celery, Corn, Dill, Kale, Lettuce, Nasturtium, Onion, Peas, Peppers, Radish, Thyme

DILL – Broccoli, Cauliflower, Cilantro, Corn, Cucumber, Kale, Lettuce, Onion, Radish, Sage, Squash, Thyme

GARLIC – Beets, Broccoli, Cabbage, Carrots, Cauliflower, Kale, Lettuce, Onions, Potatoes, Sage, Strawberries, Swiss Chard, Thyme, Tomatoes

KALE – Beets, Bush Beans, Cilantro, Cucumber, Dill, Garlic, Lettuce, Onions, Peas, Potatoes, Radish, Spinach

LEEKS – Carrots, Celery, Onion, Potatoes, Radish, Sage, Spinach, Thyme

LETTUCE – Beets, Broccoli, Carrots, Cauliflower, Cucumber, Dill, Garlic, Kale, Onion, Radish, Sage, Spinach, Squash, Strawberries, Swiss Chard, Thyme, Tomatoes

MELON – Corn, Marigold, Nasturtium, Sage, Squash, Sunflower, Thyme

ONION – Beets, Broccoli, Cabbage, Carrots, Cauliflower, Cucumber, Dill, Kale, Leeks, Lettuce, Parsley, Potatoes, Sage, Strawberries, Swiss Chard, Thyme, Tomatoes

OREGANO – Basil, Broccoli, Cabbage, Cauliflower, Peppers, Radish, Rosemary, Sage, Thyme, Tomatoes

PARSLEY – Carrots, Celery, Chives, Corn, Onion, Peas, Peppers, Sage, Thyme, Tomatoes

PEAS – Beans, Carrots, Corn, Cucumber, Kale, Parsley, Peppers, Radish, Spinach, Squash, Sage, Strawberries, Thyme

PEPPERS – Basil, Carrots, Cucumber, Oregano, Parsley, Peas, Rosemary, Sage, Squash, Swiss Chard, Thyme, Tomatoes

POTATOES – Beans, Cabbage, Chives, Cilantro Corn, Kale, Leeks, Onions

RADISH – Beans, Beets, Carrots, Chives, Cucumber, Dill, Kale, Leeks, Lettuce, Oregano, Peas, Spinach, Squash, Swiss Chard

ROSEMARY – Beans, Broccoli, Cabbage, Carrots, Cauliflower, Oregano, Peppers, Sage, Thyme

SAGE – Broccoli, Cabbage, Carrots, Cauliflower, Basil, Beans, Chives, Cilantro, Corn, Dill, Garlic, Leeks, Lettuce, Melon, Onion, Oregano, Parsley, Peas, Peppers, Rosemary, Spinach, Squash, Strawberries, Sunflower, Swiss Chard, Thyme, Tomatoes

SPINACH – Broccoli, Cauliflower, Celery, Cilantro, Kale, Leeks, Lettuce, Peas, Radish, Sage, Strawberries, Thyme

SQUASH – Beans, Corn, Dill, Lettuce, Nasturtium, Peas, Peppers, Radish, Sage, Thyme

STRAWBERRIES – Beans, Garlic, Lettuce, Onion, Peas, Sage, Spinach, Thyme

SUNFLOWER – Corn, Melon, Sage, Thyme

SWISS CHARD – Beans, Broccoli, Cabbage, Cauliflower, Celery, Cilantro, Garlic, Lettuce, Onion, Peppers, Radish, Sage, Thyme, Tomatoes

THYME – Basil, Beans, Broccoli, Cabbage, Carrots, Cauliflower, Celery, Chives Cilantro, Corn, Cucumber Dill, Garlic, Leeks, Lettuce, Melon, Nasturtium, Onion, Oregano, Parsley, Peas, Peppers, Rosemary, Sage, Spinach, Strawberries, Squash, Sunflower, Swiss Chard, Thyme, Tomatoes

TOMATOES – Basil, Beans, Beets, Celery, Chives, Cucumber, Garlic, Lettuce, Marigold, Nasturtium, Onion, Oregano, Parsley, Peppers, Sage, Swiss Chard, Thyme

GARDEN NOTES

GARDEN NOTES

GARDEN NOTES